PRAISE FOR *TEEN GRIEF*

Teens are hurting. When it comes to grief and loss, they are often overlooked. *Teen Grief* does an excellent, thorough job of getting us in touch with the grieving teenage heart and what we can do to help. Sensitive, compassionate, and practical, this book will be invaluable to many parents, grandparents, teachers, coaches, counselors, and anyone working with youth.

–Paul Casale, Licensed Mental Health
Counselor/Marriage & Family Therapist

Gary Roe has done it again. We all know how difficult it is to be a teen. Complicated by all the realities of teenage life, when grief strikes, recovery can be a real challenge. Clear, readable, and well-organized, *Teen Grief* tackles the tough topics head-on. Full of practical suggestions and exercises, this is an invaluable resource for parents, teachers, coaches, ministers, and anyone who has a teenager they love and want to help along the grief journey.

–Glen Lord, President/CEO, The Grief Toolbox;
President, Board of Directors, The Compassionate Friends

Gary has gone straight to the heart and soul, with a style that speaks intimately to those who hurt. As someone who has worked with hurting teens for over 20 years, I can say with confidence that Gary has answered a need that society has been screaming and begging for. A must read for anyone who has kids or was hurt as a teenager.

–Scott Willmore, Senior Pastor, Connecting Point Church

Grief at any age is difficult; teenage grief is a special challenge. Gary tackles a very difficult topic, presenting the complexity of the grieving process in a highly practical and authentic way through the eyes of teenagers. This is not just a book about bereavement theory; its practical advice is crisp, focused and invaluable. Another meaningful volume of hope and healing by a skilled and compassionate author.

–Dr. Craig Borchardt, President /
CEO, Hospice Brazos Valley

Teens are confusing creatures, and we all struggle with knowing how to help them through difficult times. The death of a loved one is the *most difficult* time of all. This book is a gift to those of us who love teens. It helps us find the words to help them.

–Kelli Levey Reynolds, Mays Business
School, Texas A&M University

Gary Roe is a proven voice in understanding how to navigate the difficult waters of grief. *Teen Grief* helps readers come to grips with the wide swath of grief that many teens struggle with. If you have a teen, work with teens, or just love teens, then this is a book you need to read. In very practical ways, Gary helps bring clarity and a pathway forward to the foggy reality that surrounds a teen in grief. An excellent resource for parents, teachers, counselors, and ministers.

–Dr. Troy Allen, Pastor, First Baptist
Church, College Station

Teen Grief is a must read/own if you are a helper of adolescents. Gary has a heart for kids with loss as he very honestly speaks of being "that kid" himself. I found personal value in reassessing the cumulative effects of early losses in my own life. Thanks Gary!

–Carrie Andree, Licensed Professional Counselor

Only someone who's been through it himself could write something like this. Gary's work is an immediately applicable, down and dirty, brass tacks kind of roadmap back to health through grieving. If your teen is going through this kind of pain, please read this and put it into action. It's the how-to for getting them through this and on to an incredibly redemptive future. This book is hope for your teen's heart.

–Scott Marlow, Journey Church, Lebanon, Tennessee

Heartfelt, wonderfully honest, compassionately written, and filled with stories of loss and hope, *Teen Grief* includes many practical insights to support both grieving teens and those who are striving to walk alongside them. This book is one I will share at Mending Hearts Grief Center and with many of my personal and professional friends. I'm sure *Teen Grief* will become a go-to resource for you personally, your ministry, or your practice. If you know anyone caring for a grieving teen, this book could be the best gift ever.

–Rev. Tommy Myrick, Licensed Professional Counselor/ Supervisor; Associate Pastor, Christ United Methodist Church; Clinical Director, Mending Hearts Grief Center

I'm in awe of how well Gary portrays the emotions experienced and the wisdom needed to handle a grieving teen. We respond out of love and compassion. We want so desperately to take away their pain. This book explains, in a beautiful way, that it's not trying to alleviate teens' pain that helps, but rather entering their world and experiencing their grief with them that makes the difference. *Teen Grief* is a gift to parents, teachers, coaches, pastors, and the teens they love and work with.

–Michelle Jeter, bereaved mother and author of *A Legacy of a Lifetime*

Teen GRIEF

CARING FOR THE GRIEVING TEENAGE HEART

GARY ROE

OTHER BOOKS BY GARY ROE

Comfort for Grieving Hearts: Hope and Encouragement for Times of Loss

Shattered: Surviving the Loss of a Child
(2017 Best Book Awards Finalist)

Please Be Patient, I'm Grieving (2016
Best Book Awards Finalist)

Heartbroken: Healing from the Loss of a Spouse (2015 Best
Book Awards Finalist, National Indie Excellence Award Finalist)

Surviving the Holidays Without You (2016
Book Excellence Award Finalist)

Co-Authored with Cecil Murphey

Not Quite Healed (Finalist, Lime Award
for Excellence in Non-Fiction)

Saying Goodbye: Facing the Loss of a Loved One

TABLE OF CONTENTS

Download your exclusive, free, printable PDF:
19 Truths for Supporting Grieving Teens
https://www.garyroe.com/19-truths-for-supporting-grieving-teens

ACKNOWLEDGMENTS

Special thanks to my amazing wife, Jen, for her constant, loving support. You have piloted through a lifetime of grief, consistently turning tragedy into triumph. You are my hero.

Special thanks to my daughter Lauren for her invaluable insights into the grieving teenage heart. Stay resilient, my daughter, and take the stage by storm.

Special thanks to Anni Welbourn, Kathy Trim of TEAM Japan, and Kelli Levey of Texas A&M for their expertise and assistance in editing and proofing this manuscript. You ladies make me sound so much better.

Thanks to Hospice Brazos Valley President and CEO Dr. Craig Borchardt for his support in developing resources to help grieving hearts recover, adjust, and heal. It is an honor and privilege to work under you.

Thanks to Glendon Haddix of Streetlight Graphics for bringing this manuscript to life with superb design and formatting. You are so easy to work with and your commitment to excellence makes even the most difficult subjects look good.

DEDICATION

This book is dedicated to the Wills family – Don and Sue, and their children David, Kathy, Kay, and Charles - for taking this grieving teen into their home over 40 years ago. You saved my life. I don't know who or where I would be without you.

WHAT THIS BOOK
IS ALL ABOUT

B EING A TEENAGER IS TOUGH. I'm sure you remember. I
do.
       We rose and sauntered out each day into a world of
varied and often contradictory expectations. We were young and
invincible. Our bodies were changing and our hormones were
on the rampage. We lived in the moment, seeking the next best
experience. We learned about relationships, experimented with
almost everything, and routinely made fools of ourselves in public.
It was fun and stressful.

We were on a search for identity. We wanted to belong. We
were rebels who desperately wanted to run our own lives. We made
some good decisions, and some lousy ones.

Our relationships were constantly evolving, especially with our
parents. We were growing up. We longed to be treated like adults
without the weight of the responsibilities that adulthood would
naturally bring. We cared deeply about those around us.

Life was emotional. We felt things deeply, and poignantly.
We maneuvered through the days, trying to meet the expectations
that surrounded us – those of our parents, friends, teachers, and
coaches. We were terrified of not measuring up. We didn't want to

disappoint. Despite our bravado, we were insecure inside and needy. It was all so confusing. We filled our lives with noise, trying to drown out the unwanted voices for a while. Almost any distraction that promised momentary escape from reality was welcome.

Many of us faced additional challenges. Perhaps we lost friends, family members, homes, innocence, safety, or physical health. Many of us endured moves, separations, estrangements, divorces, poverty, domestic violence, abuse, bullying, natural disasters, or death. We found ways to cope, but not always well. Some of us piled up regrets we wish we could somehow erase.

NO TEEN CAN DO THIS ALONE

Over the last two decades, I've raised four kids through the teen years, have two teens currently, and one more in the pipeline. All my children are adopted and have experienced multiple losses. All seven have lost fathers. Two have lost both parents. Three have spent time on the streets. Some have lived through poverty, violence, and sexual abuse. All of them had to navigate a host of grief-related issues. They're still dealing with some of these issues and will be for a while. They stumble from time to time, but they're moving forward, healing as they go.

I guess that describes most of us. None of us have arrived. I know I haven't.

When I look at teens today, I'm honestly staggered by the challenges they face. The needs seem greater, and the obstacles more formidable. With this reality comes great opportunity. So much of life is about grieving, adjusting, and overcoming. In an anxious and often fearful world, teens have an unparalleled opportunity to rise to the occasion and transform tragedy into something positive and meaningful.

But they can't do it alone.

WHY I WROTE THIS BOOK

I wrote this book because I remember what it was like to be a teen who thought he had lost everything.

I met loss early. Childhood sexual abuse stole my innocence and skewed my view of self, people, and the world. Both grandfathers died early. I was bullied at school. I lost friends to moves, and one to spinal meningitis. My parents separated and divorced. My mom disappeared into mental illness. I watched my dad have a heart attack, and then die a week later. By age 15, I was a functional orphan, wondering if life was worth it.

When I see hurting, grieving teens, I feel a bond, a connection. I remember. I can be back there in an instant.

I can almost hear my 16-year old voice saying...

"How did this happen? Why me?"

"How do I deal with this? What am I supposed to do?"

"Am I bad? Is this my fault?"

"I feel so alone. Maybe I am alone."

"No one is safe. We're all going to die. Who's next? Is it me?"

"Am I going to make it? I wonder."

I can sense the sadness, pain, anger, guilt, loneliness, and fear in teens' eyes. I want to help.

As I think back over my adult life, it's astounding how many hurting teens have appeared and sought me out. I believe they somehow sensed the commonality between us - soul-cracking, heart-crushing loss.

Teens came. I listened. And listened. And listened some more. As they shared their hearts, I could see the pain written on their features.

Inevitably they would ask, "Have you lost anyone?" Some extremely intuitive teens said, "I can tell you get it. Who have you lost?" If they ask for my story, I tell them. Teens value honesty and authenticity more than we realize. As I share, they feel some of my pain, though it is decades old. They tear up or breathe a sigh of relief. They might feel lonely, but suddenly they know they're not alone.

I hope they walk away a little lighter, knowing that if I survived, they can too.

I also wrote this book by request. Parents, teachers, coaches, and school counselors have repeatedly asked me to put together a resource that could serve as a road map for those interested in supporting grieving teens. *Teen Grief* is the result.

Teens are the future, and their hearts are at stake. Each one is priceless, one-of-a-kind, with a profound purpose and calling. We can't afford to allow pain and loss to get the better of them. Each teen heart is a treasure beyond description.

We can help. We must.

WHAT YOU WILL LEARN IN THIS BOOK

This book is not a textbook or a psychological treatise based on research. *Teen Grief* is written as an informative and practical handbook for adults who are engaged with hurting teens and looking for guidance, insight, and ideas for helping them navigate the turbulent waters of loss.

This book is not for teens, but for those who love and serve them. It is not an exhaustive volume with all the answers. It is a work born of personal experience and more than three decades of interacting with grieving teenage hearts. I have not tried to cover everything, but I have tried to be thorough enough to provide a wide range of insight, help, and suggestions.

Not everything you read in the following pages will be applicable to every teen. There is no magic pill, no cookie-cutter works-every-time approach. I have tried to cover what is common for most grieving teens. Read on, take what seems to apply to them, and use it for what it's worth.

Teen Grief is divided into three sections:

Part One: Understanding Teen Grief
These chapters lay the groundwork for supporting teens by discussing what teen grief is and how deep it goes. We'll show how influential teens' personal history can be and how that plays into how they live and deal with loss today.

Part Two: Inside the Grieving Teenage Heart
This section (the major portion of the book) explores the grieving teenage heart - the thoughts and emotions teens often struggle with. In these chapters, you'll get a glimpse of two teen hearts, named Katie and Josh. They are not two specific people, but rather a composite of thoughts and emotions I've heard from hundreds of young people over the years. Each chapter contains practical suggestions on how you can walk with and better support the teens around you.

Part Three: Practical Suggestions for Helpers
This final section contains information specifically for parents, teachers and coaches, counselors and social workers, and clergy or religious professionals. These chapters focus on insights and suggestions specific to who you are in the teen's life.

Most of us tend to associate grief with death. But the death of a loved one is not the only loss kids can experience. By the time their teen years expire, most individuals have faced a variety of losses due to moves, estrangements, separations, divorces, disappointments, perceived defeats, departures, rejections, neglect, substance abuse, domestic violence, sexual abuse, illnesses, disabilities, natural disasters, and traumatic accidents. These losses accumulate over time and shape teens and their thinking about themselves, others, God, life, and the world.

For our purposes in this book, we'll be referring primarily to losses due to death, but the principles discussed can be applied to any loss our teens are experiencing at any given moment.

ONE LAST THING

As I began to write *Teen Grief*, I asked my daughter Lauren to participate in this daunting project with me. Lauren's biological father died of pancreatic cancer at the onset of her teen years. The year-long treatment process, medical interventions, and caregiving at home were just as traumatic as his death. Lauren found solid, supportive friends, and good, healthy outlets to process her grief. Still in her teen years, her insights into the grieving teenage heart have been invaluable. Part of her story is included in chapter two.

Living and working with teens is an honor. They are special people, about to go out and make their mark on the world. We can help them offload some of the heavier baggage so that they can pursue their callings with lighter and more seasoned hearts. We can walk along with them as they discover how to turn what looks terrible into something productive, positive, and good.

Yes, you can make a difference - more than you realize. Read on and discover how.

PART ONE

UNDERSTANDING TEEN GRIEF

CHAPTER 1

TEEN GRIEF: "HOW BIG IS IT?"

H OW BIG IS TEEN GRIEF?
Huge.
Massive.
Bigger than you could imagine.

GRIEF ISN'T ONLY ABOUT DEATH

When we use the word "grief," most of us think of death. But grief is far more expansive than this.

Grief is a result of *any* kind of loss, whether *real* or *perceived*. Not all losses are deaths, and each loss is different in scope and impact. Some are minimal, while others cut extremely deep. Death is often assumed to be the most powerful of all losses, but that is not necessarily the case. For many human hearts, there are many things worse than a death.

Teens tend to be adventurous, hormonal, a little edgy, and full of angst. They are fun-loving, risk-taking, and seemingly indestructible. They live more in the moment than most of us. They are experience-oriented. They naturally search for the newest, trendiest, and most exciting thing out there. They are constantly engaged in a moment-by-moment quest to discover who they are and where they fit in this wacky and ever-changing world.

Most teens are tech-driven and used to having the world at

their fingertips. They are exposed daily to astronomical amounts of information and opportunity, and not all of it is good or beneficial. They routinely sift through a myriad of messages from internet radio, personal playlists, YouTube, Snapchat, Twitter, and multiple other forms of social media. Their hearts are bombarded with messages from parents, family, friends, classmates, teachers, coaches, and people they don't know. Every day, they wander through a minefield of opportunity, where it can be difficult to recognize what's safe and what's not.

Our teens are up against a lot. They live in an anxious, often troubled and fearful world. They get hit, and some losses come early. By the time kids become teens, many have experienced multiple, heavy losses. When they enter adulthood, most teens have racked up more wounds than we might at first imagine.

THE WOUNDS OF THE TEENAGE HEART CAN BE DEEP

Aubrey moved several times in her childhood. Parental job changes kept her family in transition. As she grew, she found herself increasingly hesitant to form new friendships. She had trouble attaching deeply to those around her. Separation from extended family and friends became a way of life. As a teen, she felt like a transient with no place she could call home.

Carter couldn't remember a time when his home wasn't immersed in conflict. His parents' interactions vacillated between screaming and cold, silent anger. When his father moved out, Carter was devastated and felt responsible. His parents divorced, and it was not a pretty process. This separated Carter further from his father and complicated his other family relationships.

Megan's parents were alcoholics. Her mom became depressed and morose. Her father lost job after job and grew increasingly irritable and angry at home. By the time she turned 13, Megan didn't know what to expect from either parent. She began having stomach distress and headaches. She had little sense of stability or security.

Brandon was raised without a father. His mother brought men in and out, but none of them stayed for very long. His mom became addicted to prescription meds. By dinner time each day, she was non-functional. As the man of the house, he felt responsible for his mom's welfare. He saw himself as a failure and less than a man. Brandon felt alone and helpless. He immersed himself in dating relationships, but this didn't satisfy his longings or quiet the critical voices roaming in his mind. Brandon grew angry and depressed.

Emily's home wasn't a safe place. Her father beat her and her siblings regularly. He threatened that he would kill them if they ever told anyone. Emily dutifully covered her bruises and lied when anyone asked about them. To survive, she imagined her father was a protective, supportive man that she could look up to. The story she wanted to be true became the one she told others. As Emily moved into her teen years, her anxiety surged. Panic attacks struck. She developed an eating disorder.

When he was 14, Austin came home and found his mom weeping on the floor. She shared that his father was having an affair - in fact, that he had multiple affairs over the years. She shared details and treated Austin like a peer, a trusted adult friend, or even a counselor. Austin's mom continued to relate to him this way in the months and years ahead, while his dad was less present and rarely available. Austin's sense of stability was shattered. His mother's collusion with him skewed his thinking about his parents, marriage, and dating. Austin's mom became overly attached and emotionally enmeshed, giving him the impression that she could not survive without him. Austin lost his family as he knew it.

Grace was repeatedly sexually abused by her father growing up. When she became a tween, he backed off and began abusing her little sister. Grace entered her teen years confused about life, family, and love. She felt dirty and ugly. She gained weight to make herself as unattractive as possible. No matter what she wore or where she was, she felt exposed and vulnerable. Fear was a large part of her internal world. She was treated as a little mistress, and never allowed to be a child. Her mother knew all this, and kept silent. Grace felt worthless, helpless, and trapped.

Marcus was raised in a critical and demanding environment. His older siblings were naturally talented and seemed to achieve without trying. For Marcus, everything was work. The constant comparison with his siblings left Marcus feeling stupid, slow, and incapable. The criticism intensified. Punishments came. Marcus turned his anger inward. Finally, he quit trying. His teen years were marked by depression, anger, and drugs.

Toni was a beautiful girl, but she could never seem to see herself that way. Her older brother had taunted her since she was small: "Hey, Ugly." "What's up, Ugly." "You're hurting my eyes, Ugly." Her brother's friends took up this chant. Girls jealous of Toni's looks bullied and demeaned her every chance they got. Toni began to hate school and started having panic attacks on Sunday evenings. She began poking and hitting herself and slowly graduated to cutting. Rejection crushed her heart and destroyed her sense of self. She believed the messages thrust upon her by a mean, angry, and jealous world.

Michael was in the car when his mother died. His mind protected him from the full horror of what he was exposed to. Though he was only 11, Michael felt responsible. They were headed to his baseball game. He blamed himself, and the guilt went deep inside and festered. He grew angry and depressed. He did okay academically, but outside of school he became a risk-taker. One friend wondered if Michael had some sort of death wish.

———————— ❧❦❧ ————————

These are a small sampling of some of the stories I have heard. They are all losses - deaths of a sort. Some teens have faced many such traumas and crises, while others have had smooth lives by comparison. The above examples are not unusual. They are more than common and even tame compared to what some teens have endured.

By the age of 18, many teens have been forced to navigate an incredible amount of loss, pain, and confusion. Each loss has its own individual impact, and they all add up over time. These painful experiences vie with positive ones to influence and shape the young mind and heart. Sadly, the negative and traumatic seem to carry more punch and power. As kids grow, they develop both simple and complex coping strategies to deal with unpleasant events.

The coping patterns and skills kids develop and carry into their teen years might be marginally effective, for a while. However, sooner or later these got-to-make-it-through-this-somehow survival strategies outlive their usefulness. Teens can live healthier, more fulfilling lives by learning how to grieve in healthy and productive ways. And we can help.

That's what this book is about.

YOU CAN MAKE A DIFFERENCE.

Teen grief is a bigger issue than any of us can imagine.

I believe most of the issues teens struggle with are driven by grief and related in some way to losses they've endured. Unresolved grief from past wounds is also the major root of our adult issues as well.

We all experience loss. Grief is universal. We began our grief journeys soon after we were born. All of us experienced some losses early and others along the way. To some degree, we've been where our teens are, and yet our experiences and theirs are completely unique. Thankfully, we don't need to have had similar losses to be able to walk this road together.

You are walking your path. The teens around you are walking theirs. Those paths frequently intersect and give us ongoing opportunities to do life together. You can make a difference in their lives. And they will make an impact on yours.

SOME QUESTIONS TO CONSIDER:

Most of us think of grief as being related primarily to death. Grief, however, is the natural response to any loss. What losses other than death might a teen have experienced in their lifetime?

Pick out three of the losses you listed above. How might these losses influence a child as they grow and develop into a teen?

Teen grief is a bigger issue than we can imagine. You can make a difference.

CHAPTER 2

OUR PERSONAL HISTORIES: "HOW IMPORTANT IS THE PAST?"

IN THE PREVIOUS CHAPTER, WE said that grief is a natural response to a loss, whether real or perceived. Most people associate grief with death, but it is far bigger than this. By the time teens reach adulthood, many have experienced multiple, heavy losses. If we're going to assist them, we must begin by being aware that teen grief is deeper and more complicated than we think.

In this chapter, my daughter Lauren and I are going to share some of our personal histories of loss with you. How important is the past? How influential are past wounds and losses in our lives?

More than we might think.

GARY'S HISTORY OF LOSS

I grew up in a small family with one sibling. Since he was 14 years older, both of us were essentially raised as only children. I lost my early childhood to the evil of sexual abuse. There were multiple perpetrators and it continued for several years.

My parents had a distant and volatile relationship. Raised voices and screaming were common. I lost three of four grandparents early. Being small and shy, I was picked on quite a bit in elementary school. Due to supposed health issues, I had a special diet, took weekly injections, received breathing treatments three times a day, and had to wear a ski mask outside when the weather dropped below 40 degrees. (I say supposed health issues because I later discovered these were fabricated due to Munchausen's syndrome, where a parent seeks attention by creating or feigning illness in a child). Thankfully, I had some good friends, and prized them dearly. Tragically, one close classmate died of a sudden illness when I was 12.

As I entered my teen years, my mom began showing clear signs of mental and emotional disturbance. Over time, she slipped deeper into illness and delusion. My parents separated and divorced. I moved in with dad. Six months later, my dad had a heart attack and collapsed in front of me. He never regained consciousness and died a week later. I moved back in with Mom, but several months later she attempted suicide and was hospitalized. For some weeks, I lived on my own, working and managing life as best I could. When Mom returned home, she announced she was leaving. She took me over to a good friend's house, rang the doorbell, said, "Here's Gary," and drove away. I was 15.

The early abuse and trauma caused me to want to become as small as possible. I wanted to be invisible. "If they can't see me, I can go unnoticed and perhaps escape," I reasoned. At the same, I vowed to become a pleaser. "If I'm good enough, maybe they won't hurt me anymore."

When I started school, I became a performing animal. I overachieved in every academic area. I began swimming and joined a local team. I out-performed my physical stature and became nationally ranked. I worked hard, all the time.

I put on a great exterior, but inside I was terrified and anxious. I felt confused, small, and inconsequential. I saw myself as an outcast.

"I'm dirty."

"I'm damaged goods."

"I'll never be good enough."

"No one will ever love me."

"I'll never be a real man."

"I'm alone."

These were the messages that took up residence in my heart and soul. I was dying inside and wondered when it would all be exposed and my life would be over.

How big was teen grief for me? Massive. Even bigger than I can still know or appreciate.

Teen grief was also huge for my newly adopted daughter, Lauren.

LAUREN'S HISTORY OF LOSS

I was born in what we referred to as the "granola hippy" town of Flagstaff, Arizona, the second of four siblings. I had a "Disney childhood." My parents loved each other. My siblings got along well. We traveled often.

The first loss I can remember was learning my siblings were affected by autism, which included various learning disabilities and other difficulties. I was the only neurotypical kid in the bunch. I felt a bit like an outsider. Other than that, my life was full of fun, friends, and adventure.

Growing up was a wonderful experience, and I looked forward to my future in Flagstaff with the same friends, same house, and same family. When I turned 12, my life was turned upside down. My father lost his job and was forced to look for employment out-of-state. He eventually found a job at Texas A&M in College Station, Texas. I was an incoming 7th grader, and this was not good timing. Texas felt like a new country with new weather, new people, a new school, and a new life.

Adjustment was difficult. The first few days of middle school were so traumatic that I asked to be homeschooled. Our pets died from parasites. Allergies and illnesses compounded things. I shattered my

17

arm in a horse-riding accident. Our neighborhood, which turned out to be mostly college students, was loud and raucous.

Soon after we arrived in Texas, my father's health began to decline. He developed jaundice, which eventually led to tests and a diagnosis of pancreatic cancer. He endured a heavy treatment regimen, including chemo, radiation, and several complicated surgeries. He battled pain, muscle cramps, nausea, and constant itching. It was terrible watching the physical and mental decline he experienced.

Throughout this time, I helped care for my siblings so my mom could chauffeur my father back and forth to Houston for treatment. Cancer had thrust me into unwanted responsibility and maturity. I felt as though part of my childhood had been stolen. I struggled with loneliness and depression. I became obsessive about my weight and appearance.

One day my father began throwing up blood. There had been many emergencies like this, so I assumed he would be fine. This time was different. During the night, he was moved to hospice.

I saw him the next day. He called me grandma, unaware of who I was. I hugged him as he lay on the bed, kissed his forehead, and left the room. It was the last time I saw him. He died early the next morning.

As a high school freshman, I struggled to balance a new school, academics, and family. My father's death was a severe shock for all of us. I tried to be strong for my family, especially my mother. I began having stomach distress, headaches, and anxiety.

During this time, my high school theatre group became my second family. I loved the stage and immersed myself in learning everything I could. Our director was one of the best in the nation and he quickly became a valued mentor. Then, just prior to my junior year, he was arrested for an improper relationship with a student who happened to be one of my closest friends. The shock and betrayal I felt were huge. I had lost another mentor. It hit me hard, and it was difficult to recover.

It has now been four years since my dad died. I believe I've grown a

18

lot during this time. As I write this, I'm about to depart for Baylor University to study theatre performance. I still struggle with anxiety and stomach issues. I still miss my dad. But I'm healing, and hopeful.

I shared a special bond with my father. In hindsight, I would say it is as if God compressed an entire life's worth of relationship into the 13 short years I had with him. Honestly, I thought I would always be fatherless. But my mother married a wonderful man and now I have a new father who loves, supports, and mentors me in wonderful ways. I find it ironic and humorous that he happens to be a grief expert. I'm thankful for both my fathers, and I see myself as twice blessed.

Grieving is hard work. As my new father often says, "Be kind to yourself, take your time, and breathe deeply."

BACK TO GARY'S STORY: HOW WE INTERPRET AND RESPOND TO LOSS MAKES ALL THE DIFFERENCE

Similar to Lauren, when my father died, my world stopped. If it had not been for the support of friends and some families around me, I shudder to think where I might have ended up.

When I walked through that door and into my new family at 15, I had no idea how the trajectory of my life would change. They took me in and treated me as a son. My heart began to settle, and then to heal. I've detailed more of this story in the final chapter.

During my college years, a mentor said the following powerful statement: "Gary, life is a series of losses. How you interpret and respond to the losses will make all the difference."

A few months later, he added, "It's not what you did, but what you do next that matters most now."

How I look at and interpret my losses is important. How I respond to them is always my choice. But no matter what happened back there, it's what I do next that counts now.

My new family, my mentor, and my faith inspired me to tackle the pain and grief rather than letting it dictate my life. I set out

19

on a quest for healing. At the time, I imagined healing to be a destination. I know now that it is an ongoing journey.

I also discovered that healing is not becoming what I once was or making things like they were. That's impossible. Healing is about being wounded and broken and somehow making it count for good.

We feel the pain. We process the grief. We allow the process to mature us, rather than disable us. We learn, adjust, and grow. We collect more cracks and scars as we go, but somehow get stronger as we tackle them in healthy and positive ways.

HISTORY DOES INDEED MATTER

History matters. We have all experienced loss, even from an early age. It's important to see our lives from this perspective and consider how we viewed, interpreted, and responded to the hits that came. Our personal histories shape us and still have impact in the present.

Every teen has a history of loss. Some are more dramatic than others, and some seem very severe indeed. It's a wonder many teens survive and remain halfway functional. Their pain matters. Each heart is of incredible, priceless value.

They need us. We can make a difference. You can make a difference.

Look to your own heart first. It's your most valuable possession. Walk the path of healing. As you take good care of yourself, you will have more of yourself to give to the teens around you.

AN EXERCISE TO TRY:

Consider your personal history of loss. Below is a list of potential losses. If you've experienced any of these, write a brief description to the side.

- Childhood disappointments

- Moves

- Serious illnesses (your own or others')
- Separations / Divorces
- Estrangement between family members
- Deaths
- Substance abuse by parents
- Abandonment or neglect
- Domestic violence
- Physical abuse
- Sexual abuse
- Exposure to traumatic events
- Loss of relationships due to conflict
- Bullied or mocked by others
- Other losses/wounds:
  - How do you sense these losses have impacted your life?
  - Which losses seem to have been the most powerful and influential in your life?

Consider your teen's history of loss. Indicate below which losses they have experienced.

- Childhood disappointments
- Moves
- Serious illnesses (your own or others')
- Separations/Divorces
- Estrangement between family members
- Deaths
- Substance abuse by parents
- Abandonment or neglect
- Domestic violence

- Physical abuse

- Sexual abuse

- Exposure to traumatic events

- Loss of relationships due to conflict

- Bullied or mocked by others

- Other losses/wounds:
  - How do you sense these losses have impacted their lives?
  - Which of these losses do you sense are the most powerful and influential in their lives?

How we interpret and respond to loss makes a huge difference. It's not what we did, but what we do next that matters most now.

SUMMARY OF PART ONE

HOW BIG IS TEEN GRIEF?

It's larger and deeper than we can imagine.

Grief isn't only about death. It is the natural response of the human heart to any real or perceived loss, including moves, estrangements, separations, divorces, rejections, profound disappointments, bullying, domestic violence, physical abuse, sexual abuse, deaths, serious illnesses, traumatic events, etc.

Our grief is never solely about the current loss, any more than our weight is the result of what we ate yesterday. We all have histories. When we experience a new loss, all the other losses are also there, lined up alongside. How we handled previous losses will greatly influence how we approach this one. The same is true for teens.

Life contains a series of losses. How teens see, interpret, and respond to these losses will greatly influence their hearts, lives, and relationships.

No matter what their history, there is always hope for greater growth and healing. History matters, but it does not determine the present or future. It's not what they did, but what they do next that matters now.

PART TWO

INSIDE THE GRIEVING TEENAGE HEART

CHAPTER 3

SHOCK: "WHAT? NO!"

I N THE PREVIOUS CHAPTER, WE talked about how a teen's personal history of loss can influence how they view and approach life and relationships. In this chapter, we'll begin a journey into the hurting teen's heart.

When hit by a loss, the teen's initial response is shock. They're stunned.

FROM THE GRIEVING TEEN'S HEART

KATIE

You're what? Dead?

This can't be happening. This is a bad dream.

How? Why?

No, this can't be real.

I feel like my brain is on fire. The heat is spreading down my neck into my chest. I'm dizzy. I'm not breathing. I can't breathe.

I think I'm going to be sick.

I close my eyes. I don't want to see anything or anyone. I just have to block this out. Then it will all be over, and everything will be okay.

I can feel the tears coming, welling up from deep inside. Do I hold it in? Do I dare let it out? I gasp and feel myself beginning to sob.

I cry and scream, but I can't hear it. It's like I'm deaf, blind, and dumb, all at the same time. Everything is dark. I feel like I'm floating. I don't want to open my eyes.

I want to keep my eyes closed forever.

I'm going to be sick.

Breathe, Katie. Breathe.

JOSH

What?

Dead?

Yeah, right. I just talked to you. I just saw you this morning.

How can you be dead?

No. This is wrong. A mistake. Some kind of sick joke.

I feel my brow furrow. My muscles tighten. The tension in my shoulders, neck, and head is growing. I notice I'm clenching my fists.

My thoughts stop. My brain isn't working. I blink and suddenly see the sad faces around me. I hear someone say, "No! No! No!"

I agree. No. This can't be happening.

No. This is not real.

No. You can't be dead.

It's like someone smacked me in the chest with the baseball bat. My diaphragm is paralyzed. It's like I'm trying to breathe underwater. There is no air in the room.

I can't move.

You're dead?

No, this cannot be real.

WE EXPECT MORE OF THE SAME

Life. We're used to it. We expect to wake up, yawn, stretch, and open our eyes to the same world we went to sleep in. We get up, move, go through the motions, and engage in our routine. We brush our teeth, eat breakfast, shower, and get dressed. We see colors, objects, people, and nature. We hear sounds and voices.

We expect our brains to function, our hearts to beat, and our lungs to draw breath. We expect to wake up and live in the same world we did yesterday, and the day before, and the day before that.

Death changes all that.

Suddenly, the world has been altered. Someone is missing. And the ripple effects touch everything.

For those who don't know the person who died, life continues on much as before. Their world is unchanged. They live, work, play, and relate much as they did yesterday, last week, and last year. But for a friend or relative of the deceased, life will never be the same again.

Encountering death is like entering some alternate universe. Everything appears the same but you know something fundamental has changed. An unwanted guest has broken in, abruptly busting down the door of our hearts, ravaging our souls like some unstoppable tornado.

Death is powerful. Quick. Devastating.

In an instant, our world is changed. We feel broken or even shattered. We stand motionless in the center of what used to be our life, blinking, hoping against hope that the scene around us will change and somehow go back to what it was before.

How can this be?

How did this happen?

Why?

We're shocked. Stunned. Our heart has been hit. Our world has cracked. Our souls are shaking.

LOSS ALTERS LIVES AND RELATIONSHIPS

We're relational creatures. We come out of the womb screaming to have our needs met and depend on those around us to do something about it. We learn and grow in the presence of others, connecting and attaching as we go. Our life becomes a web of relationships that forms the basis of who we think we are.

Teenagers are still discovering the world and who they are in it. Their sense of identity is powerfully linked to the people and influences around them. When someone near them is removed, their whole being shakes. When one strand is severed, the entire web reverberates with the shock.

For our purposes in this book, I'm going to refer to the teen's world as their heart-home. This is where they do life with the people around them: family, friends, classmates, co-workers, neighbors, and even enemies.

When someone in their heart-home is taken or leaves, it can throw everything into confusion. At first, they're shocked and stunned - even immobilized inside.

YOU CAN MAKE A DIFFERENCE

How can you help?

First, make your primary goal to enter the teen's world and love them there.
If you want to care for a grieving teen, your goal is to love them. The target is not to fix this, rescue them, or make this go away (all of which are impossible). Love begins with meeting them where they are, and accepting them there. It involves entering their world and being with them in their stuff.

Second, be aware that their world has changed forever.
They're stunned. Their heart-home has been ravaged and everything is suddenly upside down. Their life web is shaking.

Most of this is internal. They may look fine - perhaps not much different than usual. Inside, they're desperately trying to be okay. Their minds are struggling to grasp the impossible. Their world is forever different, but they can't process or feel that yet. At first, they're in shock.

Shock can be a good thing. It's designed to protect them from the full onslaught and reality of what happened. If we could fully experience traumas when they occur, we would never make it. Loss, trauma, and death must be handled in small doses - one small step, one moment at a time.

Third, prepare yourself to be patient – with the teen and yourself.
Grief is a process, not an event or an activity. It is the mental, physical, emotional, and spiritual adjustment over time to a loss. Time does not heal all wounds, but healing does take time.

Prepare yourself to be patient. This is a hard, bumpy, and painful road. Be patient with your teen, and yourself.

Fourth, know that your presence is the most powerful gift you can give.
We must meet our grieving teens where they are. At first, they will be stunned. Take this into account. Show up. Words are cheap, if not useless at this stage. Just be there.

Your presence can sustain them through the shock. In fact, it is the greatest gift you can give.

SOME QUESTIONS TO CONSIDER:

Have you seen signs of shock in your teen's life? How so? (Keep in mind that they may go in and out of shock many times throughout the grief process).

Rather than trying to rescue the teen or fix this somehow, what would it mean for you to enter their world and accept them where they are?

If your presence is the most powerful gift you can give a teen, what would that look like in your situation?

> *Shock is natural and often healthy in grief. Meet teens where they are, and love them there.*

CHAPTER 4

DENIAL: "I'M GOOD. I'M OKAY. REALLY."

IN THE LAST CHAPTER, WE began our journey into the grieving teen's heart. Their initial response to loss is shock. Their heart has been hit. They're stunned. They wonder what happened.

Then their minds begin to grapple with the situation. Their loved one was just here. Now they're gone. This can't be real.

FROM THE GRIEVING TEEN'S HEART

KATIE

I still don't believe it.

How can this be real?

Everyone is saying you're dead, but I just can't seem to get it. I don't want to get it. And if I refuse to believe it, maybe it won't be true after all. Maybe I can stop this, or reverse it somehow. I want you here, still here, now.

People ask how I'm doing. I smile and say, "I'm okay." I'm anything but okay, but what am I supposed to say?

How am I doing? I don't know. You're dead. How should I be doing?

I'm not okay. I'm not fine. This hurts, but I can't seem to feel the pain yet. I know my heart is breaking. I can feel it slowly coming apart. It's like some hole is opening up under me and I'm falling...

Falling...falling...

I close my eyes. Come on. Get a grip. Breathe. Be strong.

Strong? What's that?

No, this didn't happen. This can't have happened. You're not dead. I can see your face clearly in my mind. You're real. You're alive. I can hear your voice.

Yes. I swear I can hear your voice.

I'm going to open my eyes, and you're going to be there. Please...

Nothing.

I close my eyes again. I'm not ready for this.

JOSH

Everyone is talking about you. Everybody looks sad. Some are crying.

People come up, shake my hand, slap me on the shoulder, or give me a hug. I nod and try to say something. I don't even know what's coming out of my mouth. I feel like a robot.

You're dead. You must be. You're not here. You should be here.

I've seen your body. I nearly threw up. You, but not you. I kept expecting you to open your eyes, sit up, and announce that this was all a joke.

You just laid there. You were cold. So cold. No, that wasn't you. That was some dead thing. You're alive, somewhere. You have to be. And sooner or later you're going to walk through the door, smiling.

You can't be dead. Can't I just believe you're alive? And if I believe it strongly enough, who knows?

I close my eyes, but I can't get that image out of my head. I wish I hadn't seen your body. No, I will not believe it.

Yeah. That feels better. You're alive. Somehow, somewhere.

DENIAL IS A NATURAL RESPONSE TO LOSS

My good friend and author Cecil Murphey once said, "I'll always deny what I'm not prepared to accept."

Death, separation, and pain come. We don't expect it, and we surely don't want it. We stammer inside, saying, "Ridiculous! No way! This can't be true." Our world has been upended. Our hearts have been hit. Our souls shake.

We deny what we are not prepared to accept.

Denial is a natural response to a loss. Acceptance takes time and has to occur on many levels, usually in small increments along the way. Some aspects of a death or separation are easier to accept than others. We typically stay in denial about the deeper, more personal aspects of the loss - the things that our hearts for some reason have a difficult time grappling with, much less accepting. Our hearts and minds attempt to keep the deceased alive somehow, someway.

The teen years are often volatile and tough enough to navigate, even without a death or major loss. A teen losing someone they love and care about is like pouring lighter fluid on an already raging fire or throwing a grenade into an ammunition dump.

Teens are consistently monitoring their environment, struggling to discover who they are and trying to fit in and make their way, all the while dealing with raging hormones that can seem to hijack them at a moment's notice. It can be a fun yet scary time, full of stress, uncertainty, and angst.

We're all wired for relationship. Our lives are fundamentally about our connections with other people. A teen's identity is deeply tied to those around them - family, friends, classmates, etc. A death or major loss during the teen years is like being hit by a bus. They're stunned and shocked, lying in the middle of the road staring up at the sky, wondering what in the world just happened. When they come to and begin to see the reality of what has occurred, it's often too much. They can't accept it.

Denial is natural. It is to be expected, and it can even be healthy.

Denial is the heart protecting itself against the threat of irreversible damage. Denial allows the heart to slowly digest unwelcome, traumatic situations one small bite at a time.

Yes, denial can be a good thing.

As time goes on, the teen will begin to accept more and more pieces of the loss they have suffered. Most likely, they will go in and out of denial about the deeper, more permanent aspects of the death. Personally, I think we're all in denial about something. Our hearts simply can't handle all the realities of life at one time.

At any given moment, we'll deny what we're not prepared to accept.

YOU CAN MAKE A DIFFERENCE

How can you help?

First, know that denial is a natural and even healthy response to a traumatic loss.
Again, the goal is simple: Love them. Meet teens where they are. Know that they will go in and out of denial over days, weeks, and even months. Be aware that their heart at times will need to be in denial about some aspects of the loss simply because feeling the full brunt of it would be catastrophic.

Second, remember that they're hurting - badly.
It's okay for them to hurt. You can't fix this. You can't rescue them. You can't make this better. But you can love them. You can show up in whatever way is appropriate and fits your relationship with them.

Again, your presence is the most powerful gift you can give.

Third, be ready to listen, and listen, and listen some more.
You can be there, ready to listen if they want to talk, share, or vent. Resist the temptation to fill the air with words and advice.

Don't correct them. Don't try to pull them out of denial, especially during the early stages. Be with them where they are. Their hearts are trying to make sense of the unthinkable. More than anything, they need acceptance and understanding.

Be ready to listen. Their wounded hearts need you.

Denial is natural. It can be healthy, and even good. Meet them where they are and love them there.

FOR PERSONAL REFLECTION AND/ OR GROUP DISCUSSION:

"We will deny what we are not prepared to accept." How have you seen this truth in your life? How have you seen this in the lives of grieving teens?

Most of us are prone to trying to fix people and situations. In what ways might you try to "fix" a teen's grief or try to help them feel better?

What would it look like for you to enter their world and allow them to hurt instead?

How would you rate your ability to be quiet and listen, on a scale of 1-to-10 (with 10 meaning you're an amazing, fantastic listener with no personal agenda)?

What caused you to give yourself that rating?

Are there ways you could become a more compassionate and effective listener?

Your teen is hurting. Be prepared to listen, listen, and then listen some more.

CHAPTER 5

SADNESS: "I'M SAD, AND
I DON'T LIKE IT."

I N THE PREVIOUS CHAPTER, WE discussed how the teenage heart will likely go in and out of denial throughout their grief process. Denial can be a good and healthy thing at times, protecting teens from the full, crippling weight of the loss. Our task is to meet them where they are, enter their world, and love them there.

When a teen's heart begins to feel the loss, sadness will most likely be one of the first emotions they experience.

FROM THE GRIEVING TEEN'S HEART

KATIE

This is all so sad. I'm sad.

How can you be gone? You were just here.

In fact, I'm waiting for you. I expect you to text, show up, or walk into the room. Sometimes, I think I hear you. You feel so close, like I can almost reach out and touch you.

Why can't I reach you? You can't simply disappear.

Then the truth hits, and you seem so far, far away.

Dead. What does that really mean? What's that like? Did it hurt? Does it still hurt? Where are you? How does this all work? Can't someone explain this to me? I can't figure this out on my own.

I miss you. Everyone misses you. I cry inside, and outside. I wake up and struggle.

You should be here. This shouldn't have happened.

How am I supposed to handle this? How will this change things? What will my future be like? My hope feels crushed.

I don't know. The only thing I seem to be able to acknowledge is that I'm sad. Very sad.

My eyes are puffy all the time. I don't sleep well. I have nightmares. Sometimes I dream about you, which is often worse. I noticed yesterday that I'm eating less. Honestly, I'm hardly eating at all.

Then again, how could I be hungry with all of this?

Everything is about you. Missing you is painful. I want to see you. How do I do that?

I can't. And that's sad. The whole thing is sad. Unbearable.

Do my tears make you smile? Are you crying too? Or do you feel anything at all?

JOSH

This is bad. I don't like this.

You're dead. I get that. But I don't like it. And I don't understand it either.

I look at the ground a lot now. I stare at walls and people. It's like I'm living in a trance. Eventually I come to and realize I haven't seen anything. I've been somewhere else. Where? I don't know. I don't remember. It's like I blank out.

Maybe my brain is busted. I wondered when that was going to happen. Seriously, I must be on overload.

I guess I feel sad. It sucks. I hate it. And I hate that you are gone.

People come up and say, "Bro! How are you doing?" Really? How am I doing? Can't they come up with something better than that? I try to be nice and at least grin. Put on a good show. But this sucks, and faking it is getting harder and harder.

It's like people want me to be better already. They want me to be good with this somehow and get back to normal. I'm not good with this. I'm not going to be good with this, and the sooner they get that, the better.

You're dead. That's not ok, and I'm not ok.

What's the big deal? Why can't a guy be sad? Is that too much to ask? I don't think so. Seems right and natural to me.

Let me be. Dump the smiling faces. Take them somewhere else. Quit pretending this didn't happen. It did, and I'll be sad if I want to be, whenever I want to be.

I'll say it again: This sucks, and I'm sad.

Sad, sad, sad.

LOSS IS SAD

Grief is emotional and one of the most prevalent feelings we experience is sadness.

Someone we love and care about is gone. Our worlds are forever altered. Our hearts have been hit, perhaps broken, or even shattered. How could we not be sad?

Death comes with a shocking sense of finality. Our loved one, friend, co-worker, or neighbor is gone. We're used to them being there, but now we can't text, call, or email them. They're absent and unreachable. We will not see them again in this life. We got used to their presence, and now their absence permeates everything. Everywhere we look, they're missing.

How does a teen process this?

A teen's life is already in flux. They're in constant transition.

Change is part of the atmosphere they breathe. They seem to grow into new thoughts, feelings, hormones, and bodies every day. Lack of change is defined as boredom, so they seek the next experience, trying to discover what it means to be themselves and to be alive. Stability and caution often take a backseat.

When someone close to them departs, a new form of change gets introduced into their lives. This change is not pleasant. It's painful, confusing, and even threatening. What sense of security the teen has is shaken. They didn't expect this. In an instant, their world is upended. A teen can already feel out of control in life, but a death or departure can elevate this sense of vulnerability to a whole new level.

When they begin to feel the loss, sadness will most likely be a predominant emotion they experience.

OUR WORLD DOESN'T LIKE SADNESS

Unfortunately, our world doesn't tolerate sadness well. We want to be happy. We want to see happy, smiling faces around us. We want things to be pleasant and smooth. We naturally expect people and situations to cooperate with our plans for being happy and carefree.

In other words, a grieving heart will always be swimming upstream. People notice sadness and usually walk away from it. It's as if grief and emotional pain are some kind of disease and the general populace is terrified of getting infected.

However, the truth is that almost everyone is grieving on some level, and the sadness of others triggers the sadness deep within us. We don't want to go there, so we shove it back inside. We're afraid of where our sadness might take us.

Teens are already hyper-alert for rejection. Now they're in an impossible situation. They feel one thing but sense the world demands them to be the opposite. They're sad in a world that demands happy, smiling faces. Under such pressure, most teens fake it on the outside and go underground emotionally. If they felt alone before, most likely they feel even more alone now.

YOU CAN MAKE A DIFFERENCE

What can you do to help?

First, accept the fact that sadness is a natural, appropriate, and even healthy emotion for someone who's grieving.
In grief, sadness needs and deserves to be felt and expressed. Feeling sad is part of accepting the loss. Rather than trying to chase the sadness away, meet the teen where they are. Find ways to enter their sadness with them.

Second, continue to coach yourself to be quiet and listen.
Exist with them in their world for a while. Be quiet. Listen. Notice their body language. Try to see and listen to their hearts. Remember, sadness is not only okay but expected and healthy.

Third, remind yourself that your overall goal is to love them.
Loving someone begins with meeting them where they are. Enter their world rather than trying to pull them into yours. If you can, feel a little of their sadness with them. Join them in it.

Fourth, resist making it about you.
Many of us get uncomfortable in the presence of deep sadness. When this happens, our instinct is usually to run away or quickly fill the air with words that deflect some of the heavy emotion descending on us.

Resist making it about you by sharing about your losses and your experiences with sadness. Teens will see this as another indication that you don't "get it." Honestly, there's not much to be said, unless, of course, they ask. Try not to poke or pry. Try not to fix. Find ways to just be with them.

I know this is a tall order. We want to help. We want to make a difference. Most of us have to remind ourselves to be quiet and listen. For most of us, trying to fix something we don't like is as natural as breathing.

Accept them where they are. They're sad. They should be.

FOR PERSONAL REFLECTION AND/
OR GROUP DISCUSSION:

When you're in the presence of deep, heavy sadness, what is your typical response?

Imagine a teen in front of you, expressing deep sadness.

- Describe what you see.
- What are you feeling and thinking?
- Now, imagine yourself being with them, being quiet, and just listening.

When in the presence of someone who's grieving, do you sometimes deal with the uncomfortableness by making it about you somehow? How so?

Loss is sad. Accepting your teen's sadness helps them feel safe. Feeling safe is key to recovery and healing.

CHAPTER 6

ANGER: "I'M SERIOUSLY TICKED!"

I N THE PREVIOUS CHAPTER, WE talked about sadness. Someone important to the teen is now missing. Gone. That's sad, and teens deserve the right to feel this natural and common emotion. We can support them by accepting their sadness, and joining them in it as we can.

Sadness is one of the two most predominant emotions grieving people experience. The other is anger.

FROM THE GRIEVING TEEN'S HEART

KATIE

I don't understand.

Why did this happen? Why you? Why this? Why now? Why me?

This wasn't in my plan. Life isn't supposed to be this way. Who let this happen? Someone could have done something, right? Could I have done something? I mean, did you really have to die?

Did you want to die? Were you unhappy? Did you want to leave? Where are you now?

All I have are questions. No answers.

This is so confusing. My brain hurts. The more I try to understand it, the angrier and more frustrated I get.

I hate this.

It hurts.

I'm angry. Everything irritates me now. I blow up at the smallest thing. I'm annoyed all the time. I'm either mad or sad.

Great. Wonderful.

This is stupid. Come back! Turn back time. I don't care what has to happen or who does it. Someone, somewhere please make things like they were.

I want my life back. I want you back.

I cry a lot. I punch my pillow. I scream inside. I would love to hit something. Maybe I should go running.

Yes, I should go running. Now.

I'm mad at everyone and everything. I'm like a big ball of anger rolling downhill, picking up speed. I feel sorry for the people around me.

I hate this.

JOSH

You know what? I'm ticked. Seriously ticked. I mean, this didn't have to happen, right? So, why did it?

I attacked my punching bag last night. That felt really good. My hands still hurt, even though I wore gloves. I'm ready to go at it again now. I could pound it all day - maybe until my hands break. Honestly, I don't care. If it wasn't for the trouble I would get in, I would put my fist through the wall, over and over and over again.

I yell and then go stone cold silent. The anger scares me sometimes. I don't know what to do with it.

Who took you? God? If so, I have an issue with that. Is this someone's fault? Did someone cause this? I'd like to know.

46

I'm even ticked at you for leaving.

I'm a smoldering volcano. The anger feels powerful. Part of it feels good. The power feels good. I've felt so powerless lately.

I've got to pull it together. My anger can make me stupid. We don't need anything else stupid right now. We've had enough stupid - more than enough.

Time to go punch the bag again. I have to get this out, somehow, some way.

ANGER IS A NATURAL RESPONSE TO LOSS

Anger is a natural and common grief emotion. In fact, sadness and anger are the two main emotions we experience during and following a loss.

Anger is powerful, and at times frightening. Most people have trouble managing this tricky emotion and expressing it in healthy ways. We tend to vacillate back and forth from stuffing to exploding. Stuffing leads to all kinds of mental, emotional, and physical distress. Exploding can put us, our relationships, and other people in danger.

How do we navigate this powerful and potentially destructive emotion?

Here are three practical steps:

1. Acknowledge the anger when it comes. "I feel angry."

2. Identify the trigger (the why behind the anger). "I feel angry when I think about how you died."

3. Express and release the anger. Find healthy ways to get it out.

The teen years are known for being full of angst. All the physical, hormonal, emotional, and relational changes often stir that angst into anger. Many teens have experienced other losses and traumas in childhood, which can further fuel the anger and complicate their grief. When a loss or death comes, the reservoir of anger within them gets tapped, and their emotional dam can crack.

Again, this is natural. They feel robbed and out of control. The departure of someone they care about can catapult their feelings of vulnerability and insecurity to new heights. Anger is a natural result.

YOU CAN MAKE A DIFFERENCE

How can you help?

First, be aware that anger is a natural and common grief emotion. The emotion itself is not negative, but how it is expressed can be. If released in healthy ways, however, anger can lead to recovery and healing.

Second, learn to be okay with grieving teens being angry. If they allow you in, you can encourage them to "get the anger out." Here are some suggestions:

- Hard, regular exercise
- Hitting a punching bag or pillow
- Screaming or yelling in a safe, private place
- Drawing or painting the anger
- Writing it out in a journal or letter to someone (a letter that will never be sent)
- Set up an empty chair. Imagine the appropriate person sitting there and talk the anger out

Many teens might be angry with God. This also is common. Perhaps they don't believe God caused this death or departure, but they wonder why he didn't intervene and stop it.

I encourage teens to express their anger directly to God. After all, if he's really God and knows all things, then he already knows all about their anger and what's going on in their hearts. And if he cares for them, he would surely want them to be real and authentic, expressing to him whatever they're thinking and feeling. I even had one teen say, "I took your advice. I let God have it. I mean I ranted and raved. I felt so good afterward. And, you know what? I actually feel like God heard me, and I feel closer to him now."

Third, be aware of your own reservoir of anger as you try to help teens deal with theirs.

Anger often triggers anger. As teens openly express their angst and frustration, you could find yourself feeling angry in return. If this happens, it becomes an opportunity for you to express and release your own anger in positive and healthy ways.

Fourth, work on processing your own anger in healthy ways.

It's hard to encourage others to do something that we ourselves aren't doing. If we want to encourage teens to deal well with anger, we need to practice navigating this emotion well ourselves.

If you want to assist others in times of pain and crisis, focus on handling your own stuff well, moment-by-moment, day after day. The healthier you are, the more prepared you will be to help teens live healthy and meaningful lives.

Don't be fooled. Teens are watching. They're smart. They're looking for authenticity. You need to be the real thing – honest, straightforward, and caring. Have no agenda except to be with them in their stuff. Work hard on your own issues. These things earn their trust.

GARY ROE

FOR PERSONAL REFLECTION AND/
OR GROUP DISCUSSION:

When do you typically experience some anger (in what scenarios, situations, etc.)?

How do you usually process anger when it comes?

Think of a time recently when you were angry. Go through the following with that event or situation in mind:

- Acknowledge the emotion: "I feel angry."
- Identify the trigger: "When _____, I feel angry."
- Express and release the anger in a healthy way – talking, venting, exercising, writing, etc.

The next time you feel angry, give yourself some AIR (Acknowledge, Identify, Release). The more your practice this simple strategy, the better you'll be able to process anger in healthy ways when it comes.

Think about your teen or the grieving teens you know. Do you sense anger? If so, how are they expressing it?

Picture a teen in front of you. Imagine they begin to express some of their anger and frustration stemming from their loss. See yourself calmly giving them eye contact, listening. Can you see this?

Make a quick list of ways teens might release their anger in healthy ways. Consider posting this somewhere that both you and they can see it regularly.

Anger is natural and common in grief. Dealing well with your own anger can be key to helping teens process theirs.

CHAPTER 7

FEAR: "WHO'S NEXT?"

I N THE LAST CHAPTER, WE discussed how anger is a natural and common part of the grief process. The emotion itself isn't negative, but how it is expressed can be. We can allow teens to be angry, and encourage them to release it in positive and healthy ways.

In addition to sadness and grief, loss tends to unearth and stir fear. How teens view and handle fear can have a great impact on their lives.

FROM THE GRIEVING TEEN'S HEART

KATIE

I'm scared.

Who's next?

You're dead. Now I know that anything can happen to anyone, anywhere, at any time.

All of a sudden, the world is a frightening place. I notice I'm starting to tell family, friends, and even people I hardly know to be careful. I've started praying that God would protect everyone else in my life and not let anyone close to me die.

But God didn't protect you, did he? Or did he, and I just don't understand? Did he save you from something worse maybe? I don't know. I can't seem to make sense of anything.

It's frightening how little I understand and how little I control. I can't even make my own heart beat.

I don't feel safe anymore. It's like I'm blindfolded and always walking on the edge of a cliff, half a step from falling. I can feel the danger - and the terror.

I'm nervous. Suddenly, time is flying by. My life feels like it's slipping through my fingers. I feel so close to death.

Sometimes, I can't catch my breath. I want to hold everyone special to me close, and lock us all up in a bank vault or something - some place where we'll all be safe and nothing else bad can happen to any of us.

That place doesn't exist. That's why I'm scared.

Who's next? Is it me?

I think I might go crazy.

JOSH

I don't like this. You're all I can think about, and you're not even here anymore. I'm ticked, and sad. And scared.

Scared. It hurts to write that word. I don't think I can say it out loud. Too embarrassing. But it's true.

Last night I had a weird dream. I saw death. He was tall and in a long, black, hooded robe. He walked around randomly tapping people on the shoulder. They dropped to the ground, and then disappeared, one by one. Everybody I cared about started dropping and disappearing. I screamed, but no sound came. Then Death turned towards me. I tried to run, but I was frozen. He took one step towards me, and I woke up in a cold sweat. Relief washed over me, but I was shaking.

It was only a dream. Or was it?

I'm realizing something. I have almost no control over anything and have very little power over any of this stuff. Death is so big, and I feel so incredibly small. I'm at its mercy. We all are. Death doesn't discriminate. It doesn't care. It comes when it wants, and takes who it wants when it wants.

At least, that's how it seems. I wonder who's next? When? How?

Will it be me?

Part of me wants to fight and challenge all this crap. "Come on, Death! You want to take me on? Let's do this!" That feels better than just sitting around and waiting, powerless.

I noticed I'm driving a little crazy lately, like I don't care anymore. Yesterday on the highway I was just plain dumb. Matthew was with me and cussed me out for having some kind of sick death wish.

Stupid. I'm stupid. It's all stupid. I'm angry, frustrated, out of control, scared.

I guess fear makes me do stupid stuff. I have to get a grip on this. I can't let it take over, but I have no idea how to fight it off.

How do you fight a phantom?

FEAR IS A NATURAL PART OF GRIEF

When death strikes, our worlds are shaken. A powerful, seemingly irresistible invader has carried off a loved one. We're shocked, stunned, sad, and angry. We can feel helpless. The world is less safe somehow. Life is less predictable. We wonder if we've been living in some dream world of denial.

We look in the mirror and see our own mortality. We gaze at those we love and shudder. The terrifying possibility dawns on us that anything can happen to anyone at any time. We will die one day. All those we love and care about will die. Our souls quake at this. Our heart can easily be overcome and paralyzed by fear.

Like anger, fear is powerful. When it strikes, it automatically evokes a fight or flight response. We put on our emotional boxing gloves or reach for our best pair of track shoes. We prep to do battle, or to run for our lives. This initial reaction can produce some wild, unwise, and even bizarre behavior. If left unchecked and unmanaged, fear can take over and drive a life.

Renowned scholar and author C. S. Lewis put it well after the loss of his wife. "No one ever told me that grief felt so like fear."

Yes, fear is often a part of grief.

Fear is universal. As humans, we all experience it, and teens certainly experience their share.

Teens seem to struggle mightily with fears related to being "not" something. Not good enough, smart enough, or pretty enough. Not handsome enough, athletic enough, or popular enough. Not old enough, rich enough, etc. They fight to discover who they are and how they fit in. Though teens often prize songs of angst, anger, loneliness, and depression, most are terrified of being alone, outcast, or left behind.

We all fear this. Perhaps it's not a teen thing, but a human one.

Death is the great equalizer. It indiscriminately slashes through race, culture, age, gender, education, wealth, beauty, and popularity. All differences evaporate in a heartbeat, and suddenly the things we clamor for and fight about mean nothing. Our vision is clarified, and all that matters is life, love, and relationships.

Teens often see themselves as invincible or indestructible. They are young and can do anything. Death quickly shatters this illusion. The teen's heart, identity, and life get hit from all sides. Fear is a natural result.

Some fear can be positive. After a loss, teens can develop a new sense of respect for life, death, and danger, leading to wiser and more informed decision-making. On the other hand, fear can incite recklessness, defiance, and even criminal activity. The departure of someone close can result in better boundaries or a movement toward having no boundaries at all.

Fear will come. It is a natural part of grief. It's not the avoidance of fear, but how we respond to it that makes all the difference.

YOU CAN MAKE A DIFFERENCE

How can you help?

First, acknowledge that fear is a natural part of the grief process, both for teens and for yourself.
Our hearts have been hit and our worlds upended. Nothing is quite the same. Fear is a natural result.

Second, let it be okay that teens are afraid.
Give them permission to experience fear as part of the grief process. Give yourself that permission too.

Third, as you try to help teens process their fear, take this opportunity to think about and deal with your own.
We're all afraid of something - perhaps many things. Some fear death or the dying process. Others are more frightened about the losses they'll experience along the way, such as abilities, memory, or genetic predispositions to diseases or conditions. Underneath most of the these is the fear of abandonment - the terror of being left utterly alone.

How do we deal with fear?

1. Acknowledge it. "I'm afraid."

2. Identify it. "I'm afraid that…."

3. Pick an object (something that can fit in your hand) to represent the fear. Look at the object and imagine it being the fear you've identified.

4. Breathe deeply and relax, focusing on your breathing and on the object in your hand.

5. When you're relaxed and ready, say something like "I release this fear." Release the object in your hand as you do this.

This exercise is not foolproof or some sort of magic pill. It's also not a once-and-done affair. At first, you might not feel much relief. That's okay. Make this exercise a regular practice when fear comes knocking and you'll slowly train yourself that it's okay to be afraid, to feel the fear, and then to let it go. Over time, this will have big benefits.

As you practice techniques like this and learn ways to acknowledge, identify, and release your fears, you'll be better able to come alongside teens, meet them where they are, and assist them with their terrors.

FOR PERSONAL REFLECTION AND/ OR GROUP DISCUSSION

"No one ever told me that grief felt so like fear." Does C.S. Lewis' quote resonate with you? Thinking back over times of loss, what kinds of fears surfaced for you?

Pick one of the fears you listed. Imagine struggling with it right now. AIR (Acknowledge, Identify, Release) your fear, using the technique described in this chapter.

What fears do you think are running around in your grieving teen's heart?

What are some ways you can you can enter your teen's world and let them know that it's okay to be afraid?

Fear is a natural part of grief. The goal is not to avoid fear, but to respond in healthy ways when it comes.

CHAPTER 8

LONELINESS: "NOBODY GETS IT."

I N THE PREVIOUS CHAPTER, WE talked about how fear is a natural part of the grief process. Fear can be powerful, and how we process and deal with it matters. As we learn to AIR (Acknowledge, Identify, and Release) our fears, we can assist teens to do the same.

One of our greatest fears is of being utterly alone, rejected, and left behind. Few are prepared for the loneliness that often comes with a loss.

FROM THE GRIEVING TEEN'S HEART

KATIE

Nobody gets it. You're dead. Gone. Not here.

Life is different now. I feel different. The whole world is different. But everyone goes along like nothing much happened. People go to work, school, shopping, and church. People text, play, date, kiss, hang out, and eat just like before.

Sorry. I can't.

I have dreams. I can barely eat. I'm nervous. I'm sad, then mad, then sad again. I'm terrified of what else might happen.

People watch me. What are they thinking?

"Poor girl. I hope she gets over this."

"I wish she would get a clue and get on with life."

"She's such a downer right now. Being around her is depressing."

"Here comes Miss Doom and Gloom."

At least, that's what I imagine they're thinking.

Maybe they want to help. Maybe they feel for me. I know they're all ready for me to feel better. Heck, I would like to feel better.

Better. What's that? What should it be? Happy? That's impossible. Am I supposed to just forget you - stuff you in a mental drawer somewhere and go on?

It's not like I have an emotional "off" switch.

People say such dumb things, even my friends.

"It's okay." Really?

"Smile, girl. Life goes on." Yeah, and it hurts.

"I'm here for you." Really? Then where are you?

People are pulling away and disappearing. It's like I have some kind of disease. This isn't fair.

People don't get it. Maybe they can't. Maybe I'm the problem. I don't know.

I feel alone. I am alone.

I hate this.

JOSH

I've never thought of myself as a loner, but I feel like one now. People are different. Or maybe it's me. Yeah, there's probably something wrong with me.

This sucks.

I could swear everybody looks at me differently now - like they're afraid

60

of me or something. Some see me, then act like they didn't. They turn and walk the other way.

I get it, sort of. They don't know what to say or what to do. Why do they feel like they have to say or do anything?

After all, you're dead. It's done. No one and nothing can bring you back. I have to suck it up and go on somehow. That's just the way it is.

I'm trying. I feel the pressure to hold it together and keep performing. Put on a good face. Stay tough. Don't show weakness. Be a man. Handle it.

I feel like a circus animal.

Where is this pressure coming from? From others? From inside me? Does it matter? Does anything matter anymore?

Man, I feel so alone.

My life is gone. Hanging out, driving, studying, working - everything is different. Everything.

You die. You leave. Now everyone else leaves, one by one. If I don't play the game, I get left behind.

Nobody gets it. Fine. I can walk this road alone. No problem. I'll go on and pretend all this never happened and you never existed.

Sure. Right.

GRIEF IS A LONELY ROAD

By its very nature, grief is lonely. We've lost someone special. We had a unique, one-of-a-kind relationship with them. It was our relationship, and no one else's. No two people are completely identical, and no relationship is the same.

As a result, no person can truthfully say to another, "I know how you feel." No, they don't. They are not you. It was not their relationship. Yes, some can relate, especially if they've experienced a similar loss. Many can sympathize, and a few might even empathize.

But no one can fully understand where you are and what you're experiencing. It's your mind, your heart, and your life. It was your relationship and your loss. Your grief, like you, is one-of-a-kind and unique.

Yes, grief is lonely.

Each loss is uncharted territory. You had other losses in the past, but this loss is different because this person and your relationship with them are unique. Strictly speaking, you've never been here before. The terrain is different. You don't know what might be around the next bend.

The same is true for teens. Loss tends to isolate them emotionally. They've been hit, and their immediate reflex is to hunker down, withdraw, or even hide to protect themselves. Perhaps they sense themselves and their relationships changing. Some people come close, while others they counted on might distance themselves. All this can add up to a deep sense of loneliness. "I'm alone. It's me against the world," they tell themselves.

Teens are already leery of loneliness. They often fill their lives with noise and activity to try to drown it out. Someone they love is missing. That's lonely.

YOU CAN MAKE A DIFFERENCE

How can you help?

First, acknowledge the fact that grief is lonely.
Wounded, hurting hearts often feel more isolated and alone. This is natural and common.

Second, be aware that many teens routinely struggle with loneliness, and loss can often deepen their sense of isolation.
This too is natural and common. Teens are hyper-aware of potential rejection. Their life is about belonging. Loneliness can be truly terrifying.

Third, accept that it is beyond your power to make the teen feel better.
It's not your job to convince them that they're not alone. You won't
be able to. They must walk through their grief and pain and come
to this conclusion themselves. The goal is not to help them feel
better, but to love them where they are, as they are.

*Fourth, remember that the most powerful thing you can do is to show
up.*
This is so important, it's worth repeating: your presence is an
incredibly powerful gift you can give. Find ways to enter their world
and spend time with them there. Be available, as you can. Listen
well. Don't interrogate them and try not to push. Earn their trust.

As their trust in you increases, chances are they will grant you
more access to their life and heart. This is an honor and privilege.
Don't treat it lightly. Love them as best you can as they experience
grief loneliness.

Fifth, be aware that on some level you are lonely too.
None of us is perfectly satisfied. There are fantastic relationships,
but no perfect ones. We're all human. Even those in terrific
relationships feel lonely at times.

Own your loneliness. Feeling alone at times is natural and
common for human beings. Seek healthy connections. Get around
safe people who inspire and encourage you, helping you to heal and
grow. Limit your exposure to those who are overly critical, abusive,
or toxic.

The healthier you are, the more you can give away to the teens
around you. Health breeds health. Give them the best version of
you possible.

FOR PERSONAL REFLECTION AND / OR GROUP DISCUSSION:

Have you felt lonely in grief? Describe what that was like for you.

How do you deal with loneliness? What works for you, and what doesn't?

For your own health and healing, who do you need to be around more? Who do you need to be around less?

Think about your grieving teen. What are some of the ways they might be feeling alone in their grief?

Brainstorm ways you can help teens decipher who is helpful to them right now and who isn't. Be creative.

Grief is a well-populated but lonely road. We can walk with our teens while they feel alone.

CHAPTER 9

CONFUSION: "LEAVE ME ALONE, BUT DON'T GO TOO FAR."

IN THE PREVIOUS CHAPTER, WE talked about the loneliness of grief. No one can truly know how we feel. Teens often experience loneliness, and loss can elevate their sense of isolation. We can help them see that feeling lonely in times of loss is natural and common. We can walk together, even as we're feeling alone.

Overwhelmed by the emotional demands, teens can often feel trapped. They're not sure what they need. It can be a confusing and frustrating time.

Grief requires space. To process their loss in healthy ways, teens need a balance of time alone and time with people that are healthy and helpful to them.

FROM THE GRIEVING TEEN'S HEART

KATIE

Just go away. Everyone please just go away.

I'm overwhelmed. I don't know how to think about this, much less make sense of it.

I can't breathe. I need air. I need space.

Can't people see that I'm hurting? I would think it's pretty obvious. But they all seem to expect me to be okay or to be better. Maybe I'm a better actress than I think.

Acting. Yes, that's what life is. I'm an actress on a stage, playing a role. Playing a lot of roles. I may look like I'm doing fine, but offstage I'm falling apart. I'm desperately trying to hold myself together. I wonder how much longer I can do that.

It would be great if the world would just go away. But I don't want to be alone either, at least not for very long. Being alone for a bit is okay, but feeling truly alone - left behind and lost - terrifies me.

Everything is closing in. School, classes, grades, friends, family, people, life. I feel surrounded and hemmed in - like everyone is looking at me and talking to me, all at once. It's loud, garbled - like a bunch of noise.

No one has any satisfying answers. No one seems to be happy either, but then they expect me to be.

Happy. I forgot what that feels like. I'm not sure I know for sure what that is. When I smile or laugh now, I feel guilty, like I've done something evil. How dare I feel something good when you're dead?

But I want to feel good.

It's all too much. I need space.

JOSH

Leave me alone.

That's what I want to say, but I don't say it. That wouldn't be good. People already don't like how I'm doing, so why make it worse?

Why can't people mind their own business? It's my life, isn't it? I should be able to feel what I want, do what I want, say what I want. I'm tired of faking it. And I feel like I'm faking it pretty much all the time.

Being alone is easier. I want space. I need lots of space.

Life has gotten smaller. Maybe it's me. Perhaps I've shrunk. I sure don't feel confident, or strong. I feel like I've been in a bad fight, and lost. I'm sad, weak, and defeated, and I'm embarrassed about it. I'm a man. What's wrong with me?

I want to be alone. It's quieter. Nobody staring at me, asking stupid questions. But I know every time I go out the door the world will be waiting, watching, and poking at me.

I don't think I really like being alone. I don't know if it's good for me or not, but it sure does feel good sometimes. Peaceful, at least for a little while.

That peace can evaporate quickly. Sometimes I feel worse around people, and sometimes I feel better. I don't know.

Am I supposed to know?

Go away, but be there when I need you. I know that doesn't make sense, but nothing makes sense right now.

GRIEF REQUIRES SPACE

When we lose someone, our hearts and lives take a big hit. We get emotionally wounded and bruised. Things begin to close in on us. It can seem like our world is shrinking. We can feel claustrophobic. It can be difficult to breathe.

We need air. We need space. We need time alone to process, rest, and begin to recover. We need times when we're free from having to relate and to be responsible for everything. Our hearts are broken, and we need time to adjust and heal.

And yet, we need people too. We're wired for connection. We aren't designed to do life alone or walk through grief without the aid of some good traveling companions. We need time to ourselves while staying connected to others. This can be a delicate balance. It's different for every person and varies from day to day (even from hour to hour). What we need, who, when, and why is a moving target.

All this can be confusing.

When it comes to teens, adults may often get the "leave me alone" vibe. Slumped shoulders. Turned heads. Eye rolls. Defiant stares and stances. "Don't get too close." "I'm good." "Don't mess with me." "What can you do anyway?" "You don't understand me."

We must keep in mind that teens often don't know what they want or need. They're experimenting, learning via trial-and-error as they go. They tend to listen most to their peers, who are in the same boat. And on some level, they are usually testing us. "Do you care? Let me push you back a little and see what you do. After all, I don't care much for myself right now, so why would you care about me?"

Yes, we care. How do we show it in ways they can see and hear?

YOU CAN MAKE A DIFFERENCE.

How can you help?

First, know that often what teens seem to be communicating may not be what they are actually saying.
"Go away," might instead be, "Give me space, but don't go too far because I really need you right now."

They need to know you're there. Show up in ways that fit your relationship with them. Be available, as you can. Meet them on their turf. Accept them where they are and love them there, day-by-day, moment-by-moment.

Second, be aware that teens who are hurting can be erratic and somewhat unpredictable.
They have a lot going on inside and aren't sure what to do with it. A rise in internal angst, frustration, and confusion is natural and common. They are often feeling things that seem contradictory. The teen years are challenging enough, and a loss can put the degree of difficulty over the top.

Third, watch out for making things about you and your need to help.
We've mentioned this before, but it bears repeating. We want to make a difference, and we like to be able to measure progress. If we're not careful, over time this can become more about our need to feel good about what we're doing and our involvement than about loving the teen as they are in the moment.

Of course, we want progress and healing, but that's difficult to measure in the grief process, especially in the short-term. There are no linear stages. We don't move from denial into anger, from anger into bargaining, from bargaining into depression, and from depression into acceptance. It's not that simple. We can move in and out of any or all of these at any time.

Our hearts will not be easily boxed. Neither will grief and healing.

The only remedy for grief is to grieve. And this is often painful to go through and unpleasant to watch. We can feel useless and powerless at times.

Resist the urge to fix. Show up. Rest assured that the teen's heart is at work (often subconsciously), struggling to process the loss and make sense of what it means for them personally. It's an honor to walk alongside them in this journey, but it probably won't be easy.

Fourth, keep in mind that the teen will be served best by a network of people.
In other words, don't go this alone. Don't take this all on yourself. Most of us want to be superhuman, but none of us will be the sole component in the healing of a teen's wounded heart.

We all need a good team around us, especially when we're hurting. Teens are no different. They need friends and family. They would also benefit from helping professionals such as grief counselors, mentors, clergy, and physicians. Others who know grief, both adults and teens, can be especially important in the process. They need a variety of people they can interface with.

It may not be your role to set up this network of helpers, but it's still good to be aware that the teen will benefit most from a variety of caring voices. Involving all these players may not be possible in each scenario, but it doesn't hurt to keep it on your radar screen. And if you have good rapport with a grieving teen, ask yourself who they might benefit from interacting with.

Every hurting teen needs a Grief Recovery Team. If they're willing, we can help them assemble one.

FOR PERSONAL REFLECTION AND/ OR GROUP DISCUSSION:

Healthy grieving involves a balance of time alone and time with others. How have you seen this play out in your life during times of loss?

All of us benefit from a variety of voices during times of grief. Below are some people who might be a part of a person's Grief Recovery Team. List the names of those you have access to next to the appropriate category.

- Helpful family
- Helpful friends
- Grief counselor
- Clergy, spiritual mentor
- Physician
- People who know grief (support groups, etc.)

Teens may need something (or someone) different than what they are actually communicating. What examples of this have you seen?

Who might be on your teen's Grief Recovery Team? Jot their names down below.

- Helpful family
- Helpful friends
- Grief counselor
- Clergy, spiritual mentor
- Physician
- People who know grief (support groups, etc.)

Are there ways you can help teens build their Grief Recovery Team? How?

Healthy grieving involves a balance of getting the alone time we need while staying connected to other people.

CHAPTER 10

FEELING CRAZY: "I DON'T FEEL LIKE ME."

I N THE PREVIOUS CHAPTER, WE talked about giving teens space to grieve. They need time alone when they're hurting. In the same way, they also need to stay connected to people who are helpful to them in their grief and healing process. We can help them find this balance.

Loss can upend a teen's world. There are times when teens wonder if they might be losing it and going crazy.

FROM THE GRIEVING TEEN'S HEART

KATIE

I don't feel like me anymore. I'm off, out-of-sync, weird.

Maybe I'm losing it. Nothing makes sense. Am I going crazy?

You're dead. I'm not. What do I do with that? I'm alive, but I feel half-dead.

I feel crazy sometimes. It's embarrassing and scary.

I'm terrified and don't know what to do. I can't tell anybody this. Who knows what they'll do if they think I'm crazy. Lock me up? Drug me?

Maybe that wouldn't be so bad.

I still have dreams. Good ones and bad ones. You die over and over and over again. I've accepted it - at least, in my mind. My brain knows you're dead. My heart isn't there yet, but my brain keeps dragging it out of hiding and into reality. On the inside, I'm bruised and bleeding.

Maybe I am crazy.

Maybe I need help. Real help. Serious help.

My brain is there and my heart is here. What does that mean? Am I schizophrenic or something? Am I sick?

I don't want to be sick, but I feel so different from everyone else. I don't feel anything close to normal, whatever that is.

I lost you. I'm not who I was, but I don't know who I am.

How do I do this? If I'm going crazy, what does that mean? How do I find out? Do I want to find out?

Who knows about this stuff? Who can I talk to? How do I know anyone is safe enough to talk to?

JOSH

I'm losing it. My brain is on fire, and it lights my whole body up.

I'm confused all the time. Everybody else is moving along just fine while I'm stuck in this pit. I live a different life in a different world - like some sci-fi flick about waking up in an alternate universe.

Everything looks the same, but it's not. How do I function? Who am I now? What kind of world is this? What are the rules?

Sometimes I think I'm losing it. Heck, maybe I've already lost it. I don't know what's what anymore. Maybe I'm crazy.

That would be just great. You die. I go crazy. Maybe I died with you and all that's left here in this alternate world is my outer shell.

A shell. Yeah, that's what I feel like. Hard. Empty.

I can't tell anyone about this. No one is safe enough. What do they do with crazy people, anyway? Lock them up? Medicate them? Make them see a shrink?

I need to make a box for this in my brain and label it, "Crazy." I'll drop all these thoughts in there, slam the lid shut, and put it away.

Yeah, I need to lock this stuff up. I feel pretty locked down anyhow. It doesn't feel good, but at least I feel a little in control. A little.

Crazy Josh. Maybe so.

Don't think. Don't feel. Put it in the box. Lock it away.

FEELING CRAZY IS COMMON IN GRIEF

Feeling crazy from time to time is common in grief. Our world has been altered forever, in an instant. Things look the same and life goes on, but we're not the same and our lives have, in many ways, ground to a halt. It's like someone reached down and pushed the pause button on our existence. As novelist Natsume Soseki said, "In the midst of a world that moves, I alone am still."

When grieving, life is often in slow motion. We move in and out of shock, denial, anger, anxiety, fear, sadness, depression, and acceptance. Our emotions are all over the place. We wonder what happened and who we are now. We don't feel like ourselves. Death abruptly reminded us of our own mortality. Questions arise from deep within.

We can feel like we're living a farce. What is life, really?

The sheer volume of emotional upset and change is staggering. No wonder we feel crazy or like we're coming unhinged.

Teens are normally immersed in an identity crisis, desperately trying to figure out who they are and their place in the world. Then death or the departure of a loved one invades. They didn't want this. It was thrust upon them. The sense of being acted upon, powerless, and out of control can be immense.

They have been thrown into a crazy situation. No wonder they feel nuts.

YOU CAN MAKE A DIFFERENCE.

How can you help?

First, be aware that grieving people, especially teenagers, usually feel crazy at some point.
Teens already feel different, and the roller-coaster emotions of grief put them even further on the outs in their mind. They might tell you they're fine, but they don't feel fine, and they're probably questioning their sanity.

Second, know that teens aren't nuts, but are being intensely challenged by an extremely difficult and crazy situation.
Our goal is to, if possible, help them shift from, "Am I nuts?" to "How do I handle all this craziness?"

You can help them make this shift, simply by bringing the issue up. You might say something like, "They say that most people who are grieving feel like they're going crazy. I know I felt like I was nuts. How about you?"

Life can be crazy. We get to figure out how to deal with this craziness as best as we can.

Third, remember not to attempt to go this alone.
You are not the sole source of wisdom and assistance for this teen. Who else do they need to be connected to? Who else can meet and love them where they're at in meaningful ways that help?

In the last chapter, we talked about how all of us need a Grief Recovery Team. We need a variety of good, safe people to walk with us over this difficult terrain. We mentioned the following as possibilities:

- Family members who are loving and accepting

- Friends who are supportive and encouraging

- Supportive people/teens who know grief (as in a grief support group)

- An understanding physician

- A compassionate grief counselor or professional therapist, experienced in working with teens

- Clergy, pastor, or spiritual professional who connects well with teens

Again, the teen may not have access to or need all these people. It's good to keep them in mind, however.

How can you help connect teens with one or two of these people?

Fourth, know that we live in a crazy-making world.
The sheer amount of negative, traumatic, and sometimes contradictory information cascading down upon us can strip us of our sense of competence, safety, and security. In addition, we will all, unfortunately, face more losses and deaths in the future. How the teen processes and deals with this loss will greatly influence how they will handle the next one. Over time, they will develop a strategy to deal with deaths and upsets. These strategies can be healthy, destructive, or anything in between.

Here are some examples:

- Heavy exercise or athletics

- Journaling, poetry, or story-writing

- Drawing, painting or sculpting

- Prayer, relaxation breathing, meditation, or visualization

- Being mentored or seeking counsel

- Attending a support group or connecting with people who know grief

- Lying, hiding, or defiant behavior

- Self-medicating with alcohol or drugs

- Verbal or emotional abuse, fighting, or violent behavior

- Depression, despair, hopelessness, suicidal thoughts or fantasies

- Sexual acting-out, pornographic tendencies, or lewd behavior

- Danger-seeking, death-defying activities, or overt risk-taking

You're not in charge of what choices the teens around you make, but you can love them toward making the best choices possible with the experience and resources available to you. In the meantime, it's prudent to keep a watch on yourself and your own life. The healthier you are, the more health, safety, and sanity you can promote in a teen's life. Health breeds health.

Let this be your new mantra: "I must take good care of myself. I'm no good to others if I don't."

FOR PERSONAL REFLECTION AND GROUP DISCUSSION:

Thinking back on your own experiences with loss and grief, were there times when you wondered if you were "normal" or sane? Can you describe what that was like?

We all deal with the stress of intense grief in different ways. Which of the following have you experienced? Which ones were the most helpful to you, and why?

- Heavy exercise or athletics

- Journaling, poetry, or story-writing

- Drawing, painting or sculpting

- Prayer, relaxation breathing, meditation, or visualization

- Being mentored or seeking counsel
- Attending a support group or connecting with people who know grief
- Lying, hiding, or defiant behavior
- Self-medicating with alcohol or drugs
- Verbal or emotional abuse, fighting, or violent behavior
- Depression, despair, hopelessness, suicidal thoughts or fantasies
- Sexual acting-out, pornographic tendencies, or lewd behavior
- Danger-seeking, death-defying activities, or overt risk-taking

Looking again at the list above, have you noticed any of these in your grieving teen's life?

What are some ways you might help hurting teens see that they're not crazy, but rather immersed in a crazy situation?

Grief can make teens wonder if they're crazy. Their world has changed. No wonder they feel as they do.

CHAPTER 11

GUILT: "THIS IS MY FAULT SOMEHOW."

I N THE PREVIOUS CHAPTER, WE talked about how loss can cause teens to question their sanity. We can put them more at ease by reminding them that they're not crazy but are currently in a crazy situation. We can come alongside them and encourage them to develop healthy coping skills to better navigate this time.

In times of loss, teens can see themselves as being responsible for things that are beyond their control. They may blame themselves. Guilt can be a persistent and painful nuisance.

FROM THE GRIEVING TEEN'S HEART

KATIE

I miss you. I haven't really admitted that to myself much. I can't believe you're dead. I keep looking for you.

I wish I had said more. I wish sometimes I had said less and listened more. If I had said or done the right thing and had said or done it enough, maybe you would still be here. If I had been nicer and reached out to you more. If only...

Then there are the things I wish I hadn't said and hadn't done. I regret every unkind word and every eye roll. I said things I wish I could take back, or erase somehow. Some people would say these are little things, even tiny - but they seem pretty huge right now. Sometimes I dream I can reach back there and turn things around.

Did I hurt you? I know I did.

How did you feel about me when you died? Are you thinking about me now? Do you think at all? Are you alive somewhere else, or are you just gone?

There is no going back, is there? There is no going back, period. There is no staying in this moment either. Time moves on, and I must, too. But I don't know what that means yet.

I should probably let this go and give myself a break. Honestly though, guilt feels good at times. I feel like I deserve it.

Did I cause this? Is it my fault? My mind screams, "No!" while my heart whispers in shame, "Yes."

Maybe it is my fault. What do I do with that?

JOSH

I'm the reason you left. I caused your death. I missed something. I wasn't where I should have been. I didn't say what I should have. I let you down. And now you're dead.

Simple math. I could have been there and done something. I wasn't and didn't. Now you're dead, and I'm still alive. Yep, it's my fault.

I hate myself. Of course, I can't tell anyone that, or they would freak out. I've had enough freak-outs.

I didn't say all I should have. I said and did crap that now I can't take back or erase. There is no delete button here. Undo isn't on this keyboard. I suck. Period.

My grades are slipping. I sense people pulling away from me.

I get angry easily. I pop off or explode on a moment's notice. I'm ticked, and it's right below the surface waiting for a chance to spew all over the place. I feel out-of-control.

I drive faster. I take more risks. I feel like starting a fight.

Maybe I could start something with a guy with a gun. Then I could get shot and be free of this mess.

I let this happen. I could have prevented this. It could have been different. You could still be alive.

But you're not.

I suck.

GUILT IS COMMON IN GRIEF.

Guilt is a common companion for those experiencing a loss. We look for answers. We analyze ourselves. We evaluate past words and behavior. We imagine what we could have said or done that might have made a difference.

We dig a hole for ourselves, crawl in, and then keep on digging. Someone must be responsible, and it might as well be us.

Our hearts have been hit, perhaps even crushed. While we're hurting and vulnerable, guilt sees its opportunity and comes knocking. Unthinking, we open the door to this familiar invader. If allowed to do so, he will move in, unpack his bags, and take up residence. Guilt is familiar to most of us, but he is not our friend.

Guilt coaxes us to live in the realm of what-if and if-only. He focuses us on the past and what we did or didn't do. He awakens within us a desire to play God and to be in control. He fools us into thinking we're more powerful than we are. We expect ourselves to know everything, be everywhere at once, and to be able to do whatever is necessary to produce the desired outcome. Most of all, we should be able to ward off all disasters and catastrophes.

If allowed to roam about our hearts unchallenged, guilt can imprison us. It can rule our hearts and steal our lives. As a hospice patient once said to me, "Guilt is bad stuff. It will eat your mind."

Grief coupled with guilt can be a formidable combo.

Teens are already in a vulnerable place in life. They're wondering who they are, where they belong, and how to live. They typically see themselves as far more powerful than they are. They seem naturally prone to guilt. If something bad happens, they tend to take it on. "It's my fault," becomes the default internal message when something bad or unpleasant occurs. They could have or should have done something else, been somewhere else, or said something else. It's their fault.

Guilt naturally leads to anger. That anger can be focused outward, inward, or both. Guilt is common in grief, but if it sinks its talons in deep enough, it can greatly complicate and hinder recovery, adjustment, and healing.

YOU CAN MAKE A DIFFERENCE

What can you do?

First, know that guilt is common in grief and a frequent guest in teenage hearts, even when there has not been a loss.
Guilt's voice is familiar and influential. If teens have had enough experience with this invader, they can easily confuse guilt's voice with their own.

Guilt whispers, "It's your fault." Over time, they believe it. Now, when guilt speaks, it's in the first person. "It's my fault. I'm bad. I suck."

Guilt does not help. It is not the teen's friend.

Second, be aware that most teens feel responsible and guilty, even if they say they don't.
The proof is often in their attitudes and actions. Are they punishing themselves somehow?

Here are some examples:

• They are more irritable and angry

84

- They are eating noticeably more or less

- They are neglecting personal hygiene

- They refuse to have fun or don't enjoy what they used to

- They seek danger more and behave recklessly

- They begin harming themselves physically (hitting, pinching, digging in their nails, cutting)

- They begin having morbid thoughts of death, including suicide

"Someone's to blame. I'm alive. You're dead. I feel guilty. It's my fault," the teen heart reasons.

Third, be aware of and deal with your own internal reservoir of guilt. Look to your own heart. Consider your catalog of regrets.

How have you dealt with guilt in your own life? Is there still work to be done in this area?

Perhaps it's time to do some expressing and releasing. If possible and where appropriate, consider making what amends you can. Forgive yourself.

Forgiving is not forgetting. Forgiveness is saying that hurt and it mattered, but we are not going to let this mistake and the guilt attached to it rule our hearts and lives.

Guilt hinders our ability and desire to connect, engage, and love others. It keeps us from being real and authentic. It derails genuine friendship and intimacy. Guilt takes, and never gives. It is a painful luxury our hearts cannot afford.

Dealing responsibly and effectively with guilt is a wonderful gift we can give to ourselves, family, friends, and all the teens around us.

IDEAS FOR HANDLING GUILT

Here are three ideas for how you and your teens can handle guilt using the AIR (Acknowledge, Identify, and Release) method:

- Write a letter to the deceased loved one. Acknowledge the guilt you feel. Identify what you feel guilty about. Release the guilt by asking for forgiveness, and then by forgiving yourself.

- Take a notebook or journal and list things you feel guilty about. Then go through your list, one-by-one, releasing the guilt and forgiving yourself for any potential wrong-doing.

- Think of one thing you feel particularly guilty about. Pick an object (that can fit in your hand) to represent your guilt. Focus on the object. Then release the guilt, letting the object fall to the ground. Now go to a mirror, look into your own eyes, and say, "I forgive you."

You may need to repeat these exercises several, if not many, times. Guilt is stubborn. It doesn't give up easily. As you practice releasing it, over time, guilt will have less hold on your heart and life.

FOR PERSONAL REFLECTION AND
GROUP DISCUSSION:

Is guilt holding you hostage somehow? Describe how guilt is operating in your life.

Has your grieving teen expressed feelings of guilt? How so (words, body language, actions, etc.)?

How might you assist grieving teens in understanding that guilt is not their friend?

What do you think about the AIR concept (Acknowledge, Identify, Release) of dealing with guilt? How might you suggest these to a grieving teen?

In times of loss, many teens feel responsible.
Guilt is common, but it is not their friend.

CHAPTER 12

PHYSICAL SYMPTOMS: "I'M FALLING APART."

I N THE PREVIOUS CHAPTER, WE discussed the power and influence that guilt can have in a teen's life. As we learn to deal with guilt in healthy ways in our own lives, we can assist teens in handling and releasing the guilt they're experiencing.

Loss not only impacts teens emotionally but physically as well. Weird physical sensations and troubling symptoms can make their already challenging lives even more difficult to navigate.

FROM THE GRIEVING TEEN'S HEART

KATIE

What's happening to me?

I have headaches. My stomach hurts. I'm tense and nervous, even when I'm relaxing. I've been sick a lot. I catch every little bug that comes along.

I feel different, like my body is betraying me. I'm falling apart, piece by piece.

And I'm tired. So tired. I'm exhausted, all the time.

I'm young. What's happening to me? These years are supposed to be full of fun and freedom. I'm not having fun. I'm not free. Frankly, I'm miserable.

No one knows this, of course. I hide it well. My mask-wearing skills have reached new heights. I can fool almost anyone these days. Yeah, those close to me look into my eyes and ask how I'm doing, hoping to see into my brain and get a glimpse of what's happening in there. I smile and say, "I'm good," then quickly turn my head so they don't see the tears welling up.

I feel trapped inside. How long can I keep this up?

I wasn't like this before you died. I used to live. Now I go through the motions. I smile through the headaches and the stomach pain. I feel nauseated, a lot. I don't like this and I don't have a clue what to do about it. Actually, I'm too busy to do anything but keep going.

I must keep going.

Smile, girl, and keep your head down.

Smile.

JOSH

I wonder if I'm sick. I mean ill. I feel like crap. I'm tired all the time. My heart beats weird sometimes. I can't sleep at night and I can't stay awake at school. I think I'm losing weight. Nothing tastes good.

I trip over stuff. I stumble even when there's nothing in front of me. What's going on?

Everything is upside down. It's just all wrong.

My shoulders are in knots. My head and neck are stiff and tight. My chest is heavy. I can't get enough air sometimes.

Is death this powerful? Is this all about losing you? What's the deal? Everyone seems fine. Everybody else is still doing life. Why can't I?

I can't keep up anymore. I try to fake it, but it's not working. I'm limping along, slowly. I feel stuck, trapped, and paralyzed. Maybe someone came while I was sleeping, snatched my body and replaced it with this wimpy lookalike.

I just want to sleep. And sleep.

I can't think straight. I'm so different from everyone else right now. No one gets it.

I'm exhausted and alone.

LOSS HAS GREAT PHYSICAL IMPACT

Loss not only hits the heart and the emotions but the body as well. The shock and the roller-coaster emotions relentlessly pound us and eventually begin to take their toll. We aren't super-people. Experiencing new, troubling, or exacerbated physical symptoms is common when grieving.

Many experience headaches, stomach distress, and muscle tightness. Heaviness in the chest, palpitations, and chest pain are not unusual. Dizziness, vertigo, and trembling afflict many. Nondescript aches and pains, along with other troubling bodily sensations, are common. Grief-related physical symptoms can manifest themselves almost anywhere at any time, and the combo is usually unique to each person.

Grief is a form of stress. Over time it can begin to suppress our immune system. We become more vulnerable to whatever illnesses or viruses might be in the vicinity. We get sick more often.

Grief can also affect appetite. We can forget to eat and drink. Many lose weight. We slowly weaken, and fatigue sets in. Exhaustion can follow quickly behind.

Grief can greatly impact our bodies and our physical health, even if we're young and resilient.

Teens' bodies are already in massive change mode. They are growing, developing, and maturing at a phenomenal pace. Unless they are already touched personally by chronic illness or health issues, most will see themselves as invincible and indestructible.

91

They inherently think of themselves as immune to pain and harmful physical distress. As grief invades, the toll on even a healthy teen body can mount over time. Fatigue slowly builds. Minor illnesses pop up. Strange sensations roam around their bodies. Naturally, they wonder, "What's happening to me?"

YOU CAN MAKE A DIFFERENCE

What can you do?

First, be aware of and respect the impact that a loss can have on a teen's overall physical health.
Losing someone we care about is like being smacked by a tsunami. It knocks us senseless. To expect to walk away from such a blow physically unaffected is unrealistic.

Second, know that experiencing new and unusual physical symptoms can be disturbing or even alarming to a teen.
Pain and bodily distress can stoke their fears, raising concerns of serious illness or even death. They naturally wonder what's happening.

Some teens can identify so much with the departed loved one that they experience some of the same symptoms. A son whose dad died of a heart attack starts having chest pain or palpitations. A daughter whose mother had ovarian cancer begins having abdominal distress. A teen whose friend died of a brain injury sustained in a car crash starts having migraines.

When interacting with grieving teens, observe and notice new physical complaints or distress. Be aware that these symptoms may not have a purely physical root or explanation.

Third, if appropriate and helpful, remind the teen how powerful grief can be physically.
Grief can take a toll on even the strongest bodies. If they're willing,

ask teens to talk about how they feel physically and how what they're experiencing might be connected to their loss and the resulting grief. As they process their loss, most of the troubling grief-related physical symptoms will dissipate over time.

Please understand that these symptoms are not imaginary. They are not simply "all in the teen's head." What the teen is experiencing is real. They're not making it up. They feel it. Grief exerts pressure on our system, producing real physical results.

Don't hesitate to seek medical advice or treatment. If it's disturbing, get it checked out. Let the examining physician know about the teen's loss so they can keep this in mind as they check for possible sources of the teen's physical complaints. In some cases, the emotions are so powerful and overwhelming that we need medical help to manage the resulting physical upheaval.

Fourth, don't expect perfection of yourself as the teen's parent, guide, or mentor.
You will not get this perfect, so let that expectation go. Your job is to love the teen as best you can, using the resources and wisdom you have, and make the best decision possible at the time.

Don't neglect or ignore the symptoms. But do keep in mind they might be a result of grief-related stress.

Fifth, the best way to deal with the physical toll of grief is to be as proactive and healthy as possible.
What does this mean?

Nutrition. Put good stuff in. Eat well. Of course, most teens are not naturally geared toward this. Do what you can to encourage healthy foods, knowing this will impact their grief process.

Hydration. We often forget the critical importance of getting enough fluids and especially enough electrolytes. Grief stress can throw the body out of its natural homeostasis. Supplementing with the right fluids can go a long way in supporting the grieving teen's health.

Exercise. Moderate to strenuous exercise can relieve a great deal of anxiety. It also releases endorphins which the teen desperately needs while grieving. Physical training can bring a sense of well-being and peace to both body and mind. Don't underestimate the power of this!

Health professionals. Having a physician and a mental health or grief professional within your reach is a huge plus. These folks can provide specialized assistance that can make a big difference.

When interacting with grieving teens, keep these four things in mind. Encourage your teen toward proactive, healthy decision-making. Remember that you're not simply helping them adjust to and recover from the current loss, but you're investing in them and their future. You're also training them for down the road.

Sixth, please continue to be aware of any unresolved grief running around in your mind and heart.
Unresolved grief might be affecting you physically. Process what you know is there. Reach out for assistance as needed. Offload burdens from the past. Travel as light as possible. Be as healthy as you can be. The freer you are, the greater your ability will be to love teens and walk alongside them in their stuff.

What you do impacts the teens around you greatly. Model responsible grieving and healthy living. Love yourself well, and loving them well will become even more natural. The results can be extraordinary.

FOR PERSONAL REFLECTION AND GROUP DISCUSSION:

In your past, have you experienced grief-related physical distress of some kind (fatigue, exhaustion, headaches, stomach distress, digestive issues, chest pain, palpitations, aches and pains, etc.)? Describe it.

At what point would you personally seek medical input and attention for physical symptoms or distress?

Has your teen expressed any physical complaints since their loss? What kind? Do you sense these are grief-related?

As a form of stress, grief can suppress the immune system. Have you seen evidence of this in grieving teens? How so?

How might you encourage teens toward healthy living (nutrition, hydration, exercise) during this time? Be creative.

Grief can produce physical symptoms. Most of these will pass as your teen adjusts and heals.

CHAPTER 13

DEPRESSION: "WHATEVER. I CAN'T AFFORD TO CARE ANYMORE."

IN THE PREVIOUS CHAPTER, WE talked about how loss can impact a teen's physical health. Strange bodily sensations and concerning symptoms can emerge. We can encourage teens to take care of themselves physically with good nutrition, hydration, and exercise while seeking medical support as needed.

Eventually, most teens experience some depression in their grief process. This can be unpleasant and frustrating. How they choose to deal with these times of depression can be extremely important.

FROM THE GRIEVING TEEN'S HEART

KATIE

I'm tired of all this. My heart is exhausted. I'm worn out. I'm in a daze. I don't feel much of anything anymore.

Maybe I've felt too much...

Maybe I don't want to handle it anymore.

People don't care. At least, they don't seem to. They're all so self-absorbed. They don't want to be bothered, and I don't want to be a downer. Everyone else is in one place, and I'm in another. I can't seem to connect. I feel lonely.

Whatever.

I don't care anymore. Maybe I cared too much before. My battery is on low, maybe even dead. I drag around from one thing to the next, but I'm not really there. I don't know where I am. I don't know who I am.

I don't feel like I know much of anything at all.

Whatever.

I can't afford to care anymore. I have to survive.

Why did you have to go? Why does anyone have to go? Why do people have to die?

Everyone I love and care about will die and leave. And then I'll die. Or maybe I'll die first.

How depressing. Why bother with anything? What's the point of all this?

No, I can't afford to care....

Whatever.

JOSH

You're dead. I'll die. Everyone will die. So, what's the point?

Whatever. I don't care anymore. I'm not angry, just empty. Whatever this takes, I haven't got it. I don't have any fight left. How do you fight death anyhow?

You can't. It's coming. For everyone. For me.

I'm morbid today. The world looks pretty dark right now.

I have trouble cracking a smile. My capacity to fake it is weakening. I wish I could just say what I'm thinking. Wouldn't it be easier if we all did that?

But no. That wouldn't be acceptable. We have to hide to make it around here. Show up. Fit in. Be nice. Do what you're told. Don't feel. Muck it through life and then die. When? Where? How? Who knows? You're here, then you're gone. Poof.

What's the point? Do we have to make up a reason to live? Do we all have to justify our existence somehow? For what? Why?

You died. I'm still here. Why not me? Or, maybe I'm next?

Sigh.

Whatever.

LOSS CAN SURFACE HARD QUESTIONS

When someone leaves or dies, all kinds of deep and potentially disturbing questions can surface. Perhaps the most prevalent and powerful one is, "Why?"

Why him? Why her? Why me? Why us? Why now?

Why did they...? Why didn't they...? Why did I...? Why didn't I...?

Why?

"Why?" seems to be the catch-all, ultimate question behind all the others. It keeps popping up. It circles back around, again and again.

Someone is gone. A strand of our life-web has been severed, perhaps forcefully. Our entire web trembles. The shock, sadness, anger, confusion, and anxiety wear us down. Grief takes its toll. Our fuel gauge is in the red. Our batteries are failing, and there is no charging station in sight.

We sigh. Our shoulders slump. Our feelers shut down. We go internal. We begin wondering about many things. The incessant questioning is exhausting. Finally, we've got nothing left. We power down. We shut off. We quit.

"Whatever."

Teens already say this a lot. Teens can feign apathy about things they consider unreasonable, painful, or scary. Inside, however, most really do care. Deeply. It matters greatly to them what happens, how, when, and to whom. No one wants strands of their web severed.

Teens reason, "That kind of tragic, bad stuff happens to other people." When it happens to them, it is shocking and terrifying. It feels unfair, unjust, or mean. Questions abound. Their level of angst rises. Life can seem random and meaningless. "What's the point?" is a natural conclusion.

Experiencing some depression in the grieving process is natural and common. Sadness descends. Motivation disappears. We withdraw and hide a little more than usual. We can feel hopeless and meaningless. Perhaps we have trouble getting out of bed. The color has faded from life.

Most grief-related depression is situational and temporary. As we continue to process the grief involved, in time, the extreme heaviness will begin to lift.

YOU CAN MAKE A DIFFERENCE.

What can you do?

First, be aware that experiencing some temporary depression is natural and common in a time of loss.
The severing of a strand in the teen's life web can exact a large toll over time. Even a teen's battery can be drained. A sense of emptiness can be the result.

When this temporary depression strikes, here are a few things you or your teen can do:

- Intentionally get out among people (a movie, restaurant, play, the mall, church, etc.).

- Reach out and help someone. Volunteer. Serve (church, food bank, civic organization, health organization, etc.).

- Talk to someone you trust (friend, teacher, coach, therapist, mentor, minister, grief counselor) about how you're feeling and thinking. This can make a bigger difference than we realize.

- Write it out in a journal or letters. Try to get what's going on inside down on paper. This helps express our emotions and process our grief.

Consistently taking simple actions like these can help alleviate temporary situational depression over time.

Second, remind yourself again that the best thing you can do for the teen is to love them.
Meet them where they are and be with them in their stuff, whatever that means for your personal relationship and connection with them. Again, words are overrated. They don't need speeches or lectures. Learn to restrain yourself, be quiet, and listen. Listen past their words and try to hear their hearts.

This time can be scary for us. We want to confront this depression and drive it far from their minds and lives. We don't want them to be experiencing this. We want them to be our version of healthy, happy, and productive.

We must remember that now is not forever. At present, our teen is hurting. They are feeling some deep and scary things. We support them best by being safe and dependable. They need constants during all this upheaval. Enter their world and provide listening ears, open hearts, unwavering support, and healthy boundaries.

Third, guard your own heart and be aware of your own triggers.
It's not unusual for a teen's apathy and depression to open a Pandora's box of your own thoughts and emotions.

When we see a teen in distress, we want to rescue, fix, and deliver them. We naturally want them safe, happy, and vibrantly alive. We want them free to pursue their dreams (which we naturally often confuse with our dreams for them). We want them to be successful, respectful, and wise.

Teens are aware we have these expectations, whether they say so or not. No matter how they act, deep down most teens want to please their parents and adults they respect. Almost every teen I've talked with fears being a disappointment to those around them.

Be aware of your own fears. Process them as best you can. Don't put your stuff on the teen. Handle your own issues well, and you'll be more able to walk with teens in theirs.

Fourth, don't try to do this alone. Involve some good, safe people.
You need a team, just like your teen needs one. Friends, family, and safe people. Teachers, coaches, and school counselors. Physicians, spiritual mentors, and grief professionals.

Observe. Listen. Be aware of and watch for warning signs. Seek good resources. Love them as best you can.

Fifth, be aware of warning signs that depression is becoming a chronic, serious issue.
Here are some warning signs to watch out for:

- They don't get out of bed.

- They isolate from other people and activities.

- They fall into addiction or self-medicating behavior.

- They are non-functional when it comes to daily routine life.

- They have thoughts of harming themselves.

If you see these signs emerging, it's time to seek professional help immediately. Reach out to a physician, grief counselor, social worker, therapist, or minister. Make the contact. Get their input. If the teen is willing to talk to them, go ahead and set it up. Get them there.

Again, you are not God, and you will not get this perfect. Meet teens where they are. Listen well. Love them as best you can. Make the best, most well-informed decisions possible given what you know and the resources you have. Breathe deeply, and take care of yourself along the way.

FOR PERSONAL REFLECTION AND
GROUP DISCUSSION:

Have you experienced some depression in times of loss? Describe how it felt and what that was like for you.

When you encounter depression in a grieving teen, how do you respond inside? Are there specific concerns or fears that surface at these times?

Look over the suggestions for handling temporary grief-related depression. Do any of these seem to fit where your grieving teen is? How might you encourage them to move toward this?

Every teen needs a diverse group of people as part of their healing team. Is there someone you trust that you want to involve in this process of helping this teen recover, adjust, and grow?

If you see warning signs of more on-going chronic depression, what would be your plan of action?

Some temporary depression is common in grief.
Support your teens where they are, and be aware of
the warning signs of something more serious.

SUICIDE

WHEN WE CONTEMPLATE TEEN GRIEF, we would be remiss if we didn't specifically address the topic of suicide.

As a pastor and chaplain, I've officiated at more than ten suicide funerals in the last four years. All were heartbreaking and gut-wrenching. As I gazed into the eyes of hundreds of shocked, confused, sad, and angry friends and family, I was painfully aware there was nothing I could say or do to reverse these tragedies. The victims in these cases are not only the deceased but all who knew and loved them. Addressing the topic of suicide at these venues was difficult and highly emotional, but necessary and healthy.

The topic may be frightening, but for the sake of our teens, we must go there.

Here are some recent statistics:

- Suicide is currently the third most common cause of death among teens, coming behind accidents and homicides.

- The United States averages just under 5,000 teen suicides per year (12 per day), with almost 600,000 attempts.

- 1 in 5 high school students report that they have "seriously considered suicide" at some point. Almost 160,000 teens each year receive medical care for self-inflicted injuries.

- 80% of teen suicide deaths are males.

- Almost half of all teen suicides involve a firearm, while 40% are due to suffocation (such as hanging)

(Stats from www.statisticbrain.com)

Yes, teen suicide is something to be aware of. And for most of us, that's terrifying.

WHAT CAN YOU DO?

First, be aware of the warning signs.

Teenage suicide isn't caused by any one factor, but usually by many influences over time. Below are some common risk factors. The more factors that are involved, the greater the suicide risk.

- Chronic depression. If a teen is dealing with ongoing, clinical depression, this puts him or her at a higher risk.

- A previous suicide attempt. This is not new for them.

- Current talk of suicide. They express a desire to die or "go be with someone" who is deceased.

- A suicide plan. They have thought about and considered a means to take their own life.

- Giving away things that are special to them. The teen may be getting their affairs in order.

- Giving the impression that they won't be around much longer. These hints can be the teen's way of saying goodbye.

- Other suicides around them. If other teens or family members have taken their own lives, the risk increases.

- Access to firearms. Since almost half of all teen suicides involve firearms, having access to a weapon can be a big factor.

- Alcohol or drug use, especially if this increases. Substance abuse can embolden the teen, ease fears of suicide, and fog rational decision-making.

- Prior mental health issues, such as bipolar disorder, major depressive disorder, eating disorders, schizophrenia, and post-traumatic stress disorder can be contributing factors.

- Sexual and physical abuse. Violations and loss of innocence through victimization can skew thinking, behavior, and relationships. Feeling dirty, unwanted, and like damaged goods can be powerful.

- Social rejection. The consistent loneliness of being an outcast can cause a teen to wonder why they're here.

- Divorce or parental conflict. Guilt, shame, anger, and hopelessness can invade in times of family conflict and separation. The teen can feel responsible.

- Illness or disability. Physical pain, disease, or deformity can evoke worthlessness and shame. Teens can look for a way out of this misery.

If some of these factors are already in play, the death of a loved one can shove the teen further along the path of wondering if life is worth it. When the pain is great, some look for a way out.

Be aware of these factors. Pay attention. Observe.

Second, don't hesitate to bring up the subject: "Are you thinking about harming yourself? Are you considering suicide?"
Asking doesn't put the idea in the teen's head. If you've observed any of the usual warning signs, most likely they're already thinking about it. Neither does talking about suicide increase the risk.

Third, remove and eliminate (if possible) the teen's access to firearms or other weapons.

Fourth, if they are expressing current thoughts of suicide and a plan, do not leave the teen alone.
Talk of suicide is not something to keep secret, even if the teen pleads for you to do so. Get help immediately. "Let's talk to someone who can help. Let's call the crisis line now."

Important resources to have at your fingertips:

- National Suicide Prevention Lifeline

  1-800-273-TALK - https://suicidepreventionlifeline.org/

- Society for the Prevention of Teen Suicide

  http://www.sptsusa.org/

- Suicide Prevention - Youth.Gov

  http://youth.gov/youth-topics/youth-suicide-prevention

- Suicide Prevention App.

  http://www.suicidepreventionapp.com

CHAPTER 14

WONDERING: "WHAT'S NEXT?"

I N THE PREVIOUS CHAPTER, WE talked about how teens often experience temporary situational depression during times of loss. This is natural and common. We can walk with them through this emotional valley while watching for warning signs of the more chronic, serious depression that can descend upon some.

At some point, as teens process their grief, things begin to turn around. They begin to look forward again instead of merely at the past. They wonder "What's next?"

FROM THE GRIEVING TEEN'S HEART

KATIE

I'm finally getting it. Things are different. I can't go back. I can't turn back time. I can't undo anything.

You're dead. Things will never be the same. I don't like it, but I'm starting to accept it. Maybe.

Then I find myself looking for you again. It's like some sort of reflex of my heart. But I'm doing that less and less now.

I hope I don't forget you. I thought that was impossible, but now, I don't know. I don't think of you near as much now. Is that okay? Are you offended? Are you thinking anything at all?

I'm starting to smile again too. I feel guilty when I realize it, but I have to admit that it feels good. Really good. I even laugh some. I like to think you would want me to smile and laugh. Maybe you're even smiling with me. I hope so.

I'm talking more. I'm less afraid. I feel a little calmer, a little less anxious. I no longer feel like I'm in a deep pit, frantically scrambling to get out. I can breathe better. There seems to be more oxygen in the air around me. Perhaps my heart is coming back to life. A part of me died with you, and the rest of me is ready to find a way to live again. Maybe it's possible to miss you and still be happy, or to at least be somewhat okay.

I don't want to leave you behind, but I sense I need to say goodbye to you somehow. I'll always miss you. You will always have a place in my heart. I'll live on, carrying you inside me. I'll talk about you, and smile. And if I end up crying, so what?

Everyone dies, don't they? But I'm not sure that everyone really lives. I want to live.

Yes, I want to live.

JOSH

Things are changing. Again. I can feel it. The change is in me.

I'm waking up. I've been living a nightmare. Someone reached in and pulled my heart out through my throat. My chest has been hollow and empty ever since.

Somehow, my heart has returned. I don't know how, and I'm not sure when. But it's beating again. I can feel it. I'm alive.

Yes, you're dead. That's finally sinking in. The world is still spinning. I'm still breathing. I'm still here. I want to be here.

I feel different now. Maybe I matured a little - perhaps a lot. Death can do that, I guess. Why does someone have to go for us to appreciate who and what we have left? Why does someone have to die in order for us to see the beauty and power of life?

I'm smiling again. I laugh occasionally. I can taste my food. I'm sighing less.

I'm starting to talk again. People are coming up and hugging me, saying stuff like, "Dude, welcome back! We missed you!"

I'm glad to be back. Yeah, I'm different. I feel like I've only got one leg, but I'm alive - and glad to be alive. I wish you were here, but I know that's not going to happen. I'll find a way to miss you but still live.

It's time to make all this count somehow. I don't know how, but I'm determined.

Life can still be good. And I can make it so.

LOSS CHANGES OUR WORLD - AND US.

Loss changes things. It alters our world and impacts how we see ourselves, life, others, and even God. As we process and move through the grief, we discover over time that we are not the same people anymore.

Some say that loss doesn't change us, but rather it reveals us - who we really are inside. The way we choose to grieve does indeed show our hearts and what's happening inside us. Severe stress surfaces the best and worst in us - and everything in between.

We stumble along. We falter and fall. Sometimes we painstakingly crawl forward, inch by inch. At our most painful moments, perhaps all we can do is lie there stunned and paralyzed, hoping that help will descend upon us from somewhere.

The world is different. We're wired for connection, and someone is missing. Our life web has been struck. A strand has been severed. We wince, writhe, and struggle. We grieve.

And as we grieve, over time we begin to recover, adjust, heal, and grow.

111

Teens are already deeply immersed in a struggle to figure out who they are. A loss can feel like a grenade going off in an already unstable existence. On the other hand, a close loss, though tragic and unwanted, can stimulate maturity and growth that sets the teen up for greater relational and life success down the road.

As they process their grief, they will move past "What's the point?" to "What's next?" They begin to embrace life again, hungry to live with deeper meaning. A death or departure can catapult teens forward to live with greater purpose. They want to make a difference.

Yes, a devastating loss has the potential to crush the teen's heart and strip them of hope. The teen can't afford to let this happen, and neither can we. Death and disaster can be turned around and used to stoke the fires of deeper, more powerful living.

Teens can find ways to use their grief, rather than letting their grief use them. Grief can become the fuel that drives them forward to make more of a difference than they ever dreamed. Finding ways to turn their grief to good can be the teen's secret weapon in the healing process.

YOU CAN MAKE A DIFFERENCE.

What can you do?

First, be aware that loss can drive a teen's heart in many directions.
Loss can be paralyzingly painful. It can shock a teen's soul and cause them to career off the rails into destructive pathways. Tragic events can also be used, however, to help them think deeply about life, love, and purpose.

Second, if the teen you're working with seems to be struggling and not adjusting, don't despair.
Many teen hearts have been hit multiple times and in such a way that it appears that loss has gotten the better of them. They're not

coping well. Maybe they're acting out or diving headlong into addictions or questionable activities. Perhaps anxiety, depression, or other mental or emotional issues taken over. Maybe they are tottering on the edge of overtly destructive or even criminal behavior.

Helping some teens may seem like a solo climb of Mount Everest. Almost any climb is doable, however, if we take it one step at a time.

Third, no matter where the teen is in their grief journey, or how many losses they've had, showing up and loving them where they are can have a tremendous impact.
Even in cases that look bleak, there is always hope. I believe that no heart is ever beyond reach. No matter where the teen is, love them by meeting them where they are. Show up. Listen. Try to hear the pain and broken heart behind the words. Many teens have never had someone sit down and care enough to actually listen. It may take time to gain their trust, but it will be worth it.

Fourth, realize that there are some teens who may be beyond your reach.
There are some teens who will never trust you. You're not in control of this. You are only in control of how you approach them, and what you choose to think, say, and do. Their responses are their own. If a teen chooses to walk away from you, please remember that it's not all about you. In fact, it may not be about you at all. It's about them, their lives, their history of loss, and their hearts.

Fifth, watch out for perfectionism.
Perfectionism doesn't work, and it threatens relationships. Trying to get it perfect will hinder you from loving. Show up. Be available. Meet them where they are and love them as best you can.

Perfectionism will not help you process your own grief issues either. Many of us tend to be hard on ourselves, wishing we could do more, be more, have more impact, make more of a difference. As we've said before, rather than accepting our humanness, we tend to want to play God. We seek to maneuver, manipulate, and control. We want to alter situations, heal hearts, and transform lives. When we try to control anyone or anything, we make things about us, and at that point, we cease to truly love.

We trip and stumble along. We fail often, but hopefully, we fail forward, learning how to receive and give acceptance, respect, and love. We make mistakes, learn from them, and hopefully engage other hearts better over time. We must become extremely good at forgiveness - of both others and ourselves.

Release mistakes quickly. Process your own issues and grief well. Take good care of and guard your own heart. Make sure you are adjusting, healing, and growing. Be kind to yourself, and very patient with yourself.

Grief is not a sprint but a marathon. It is not an event or a to-do list. Adjustment, recovery, and healing are all processes. Time may not heal all wounds, but healing does take time.

Breathe deeply, and help your teen do the same.

FOR PERSONAL REFLECTION AND GROUP DISCUSSION:

Look back at a few of your own losses. Can you see some good coming out of these situations? How so?

What would you say you've gained from your losses? How have you grown and matured as a result of loss?

Have you seen growth and maturity in your teen as a result of going through loss? How so? (If not, don't despair. They may not be at the point where you can observe healing and growth yet).

Teens want to make a difference. They want their lives to count. How can you help them use this loss and their grief to give them a greater sense of purpose and meaning in life? How might they make their pain and grief count?

Look again at the following statements. Which of these do you struggle with? Are there healthy adjustments you want to make?

- Release mistakes quickly.
- Process your own issues and grief well.
- Take good care of and guard your own heart.
- Make sure you are adjusting, healing, and growing.

Meeting grieving teens where they are and walking with them is not easy. Be patient with both them and yourself.

CHAPTER 15

HOPE: "I'M GOING TO MAKE IT."

IN THE PREVIOUS CHAPTER, WE discussed how the teen's heart will turn back toward life and living as they process their grief. Their hearts will begin to settle and they start looking forward again. We can encourage them to use their grief to live with more purpose and meaning than ever before.

As grieving teens begin to re-engage in life, they need to find ways to remember and honor departed loved ones. Rather than moving on without them, teens learn to move on with their loved ones, but in new ways.

FROM THE GRIEVING TEEN'S HEART

KATIE

I'm going to make it. I wondered about myself for a while there. I thought my life was over. My heart was crushed. But somehow, I'm ready to live again.

I don't want to simply live. I want to live better. I want your death to count. I want my life to count.

I was worried about forgetting you. I realized last week that I can keep that from happening simply by deliberately remembering you. I will talk about you. I will share my memories. I will tell your story over and over again. I will share pictures, video, and anything else I have. I want others to know you. I want them to know you through my eyes.

Maybe some of us who loved you can get together and do something even better. A party perhaps? Buy you a card. Eat your favorite foods. Watch some movies you loved. Tell stories about you and share our memories. Why not? Why don't we do more of this kind of thing when someone dies? Are we afraid of tears?

I've learned that when I fear tears, I also keep myself from smiling and laughing. They all go together, just usually not at the same moment.

I have a few special things, too - items that remind me of you. They're not worth anything to anyone else, but to me they're priceless. I'll treasure these things and keep them safe. I'll look at them often, and remember.

And why do special days only have to bring sadness? Your birthday, Thanksgiving, Christmas, New Years, and the day you died. Can't we celebrate you on these days too? It's about time we gave death, sadness, and depression some good competition.

I'm determined to remember and honor you. You made a difference in my life, and I'll never forget you. I'm grateful for you, and I want to live that way.

I'll remember and celebrate. You're worth it. I'm worth it. We're worth it.

JOSH

It's time to move on, but I refuse to leave you behind. I can't. You're coming with me because you're a part of me. I take you with me wherever I go. When people see me, they're seeing a little of you too.

So, I'm not moving on without you, but with you. Your influence is still here, and I'm going to make sure it stays.

I find myself saying your name lately, out loud. When I thought of you, I used to cry or get angry. Now I speak your name and smile. I see you inside my head. I speak your name to others who knew you and smile. They grin and smile back. Sometimes, they say your name too.

A name is powerful. It's so short, but it can say so much.

Your birthday is coming up. I want to speak your name a lot that day. I'll say it on the day you died too, and on Christmas, Thanksgiving, Easter, and every other special day on the calendar. I'll speak your name, over and over. I'll share stories and memories. I'll listen to others as they share memories and stories of you. Together, we will keep you alive, if only in our hearts and minds.

Weird. You're dead, but you're here. You're gone, but your influence remains. I can live remembering you, even while I'm missing you. I don't like it, but I'll work with it. It is what it is. I'll fight for you, for your name, for your memory.

I will honor you. I will live well. I will live for both of us.

SAYING GOODBYE MAY NOT BE WHAT WE THINK

Saying goodbye is important. How we process our grief, adjust, and recover matters. Accepting the death of our loved one doesn't mean forgetting or abandoning them. In fact, as we grieve in healthy ways, we end up remembering those who have died and celebrating their lives and influence.

In other words, saying goodbye sometimes means saying hello in new ways. We commit ourselves to remember. We resolve to honor them.

We speak their names.
We tell their stories.
We remember and honor them on special days.
We live their legacy.

We use our grief to love them. After all, our love for them didn't die. We loved them, and we love them still. This is why loss is painful and grief is challenging. Deaths and departures can break our hearts. As we learn to grieve in healthy and positive ways by processing our emotions well and including others who are helpful to us in our recovery and healing, our Humpty Dumpty hearts somehow begin to come together again. Perhaps a few pieces are missing. Our cracks are clearly visible. Our once broken hearts can heal to become stronger than ever before, but they are not the same. A strand of our life-web has been severed, and we are forever different.

We say goodbye to loved ones, while at the same time finding new ways to love and honor them in our hearts, words, and actions.

Teens are already looking to make sense of their world and discover their place in it. Their closest connections, usually friends and family, are hugely important in this process. When a strand of their life web is severed, they naturally hurt and grieve. As they grieve, they seek to find meaning in this loss. They search for answers and eventually find ways to give meaning to the death of their loved one. They remember. Stories and memories become priceless. Photos, videos, and certain possessions become treasures.

As they encounter shock, sadness, anger, anxiety, fear, and depression, teens are unknowingly putting their own hearts back together again (with the assistance of other influences and people around them, of course). They feel their grief, and then turn it around and use it.

YOU CAN MAKE A DIFFERENCE.

What can you do?

First, remember that your task is to walk alongside the teen in their stuff, accepting and loving them where they are.
Your job isn't to fix, heal, and make them better. All these are beyond you. You're not that powerful.

Second, remember the incredible difference you can make if you simply show up in the teen's life and make yourself available.
It's their heart and their life, and it's an honor to be included. If they share their heart with you, they're giving you access to a great treasure - their most prized and important possession.

120

Take their heart seriously. Handle it with utmost care. It is deeply fragile and responds well to being listened to and understood. If the teen's heart feels safe, healing and recovery become possible (and even likely).

Show up. Be available. Listen. Seek to understand. Be safe.

Third, you can encourage them as they use their grief to remember and honor the relationship they lost.
You can encourage them to...

- **Speak the name of their loved one.** There is power in a name. Saying it out loud can be scary, and deeply meaningful. Speaking their name is part of remembering their loved one.

- **Tell the stories of their loved one.** Invite teens to share memories. Encourage them to tell their loved one's story. This will bring tears, smiles, and healing. It may not always be comfortable, but it can be cathartic and encouraging.

- **Honor their loved one on special days.** Our calendars are littered with days that remind us of our losses - birthdays, anniversaries, Thanksgiving, Christmas, Easter, Valentine's Day, etc. You can assist teens in making these days count. Help them make simple plans to remember and honor their loved ones on these days.

- **Live their loved one's legacy.** We remember people by engaging in service, perhaps even in a cause that was important to them. We give in their name. We can encourage and inspire teens to consider what it would mean to honor their loved one with how they live their daily lives. This almost always results in serving and giving. Such things expand our hearts, bring perspective, and promote healing.

Life is worth living. As teens turn their attention back toward the present and the future, we can help them remember their loved ones in healthy and healing ways.

FOR PERSONAL REFLECTION AND
GROUP DISCUSSION:

Take a moment and think of a loved one who has died. Speak their name. Say it again. What came to mind as you did this?

Think of a time that you shared a memory or story of a deceased loved one. Who and what was it about? Describe how you felt when you shared it.

How can you encourage teens to speak the name of their loved one and share memories of them? What ideas come to mind?

What are some simple ways to remember and honor loved ones on special days (birthdays, death anniversaries, Thanksgiving, Christmas, etc.)? Brainstorm some ideas here.

How might you assist a teen in making a simple plan to celebrate their loved one on an upcoming holiday?

As you show up and meet your grieving teen where they are, the results can be extraordinary. Helping them tell their story and honor their loved one can bring healing over time.

SUMMARY OF PART TWO

WHEN LOSS HITS THE TEENAGE heart, the impact is immense. Shock, denial, sadness, and anger invade, making already challenging days even more difficult to navigate. Many battle with fear, guilt, and depression. Some feel like they're losing it mentally or falling apart physically. Some even wonder if life is worth it.

Loss and the resulting grief touches every part of their being – heart, mind, body, and soul. Their world is changing, and many of the alterations are disturbing, unwanted, and painful. The loneliness of the grief process can be intense, and teens can begin to question whether they're going to make it through this intact.

We can make a difference. We can enter their world and meet teens where they are. We can be safe people who listen and love rather than trying to fix or control. We can choose to walk with them in their stuff, feel some of their pain, and win their trust on a deeper level.

We can be real and authentic about our own losses and grief, helping teens realize that they are not alone, not crazy, and that they can survive this.

As we love them where they are in their grief, teens can find the courage and strength to move through their roller-coaster emotions and live with a new sense of purpose and meaning. Loss can be devastating, but it can be turned into an opportunity to rise above, overcome obstacles, and serve other hurting, wounded hearts.

Grief is tough, but it can be used for good.

Yes, we can make more of a difference than we realize.

PART THREE
PRACTICAL SUGGESTIONS FOR HELPERS

CHAPTER 16

FOR PARENTS

P ARENTING IS NOT FOR SISSIES. It takes guts, courage, faith, and loads of patience.

Watching our teens hurt is heartbreaking. We want to fix it and drive the pain far, far away from them. We want to insulate and shield them from anything else terrible or disastrous. We want to protect them from themselves and erect whatever fences necessary to keep them from careening out of control and doing damage to themselves and their futures.

If we have other kids, we're equally concerned about them. The sheer weight of responsibility can be daunting and even debilitating. We wonder how we're going to manage it all. We can feel out of control, out of our depth, and helpless. We can feel powerless in the face of the onslaught of the harder parts of life on us and our kids.

In addition, single parents often have no partner with whom to process, evaluate, and make decisions. The loneliness can be extreme and heavy. This can also happen with couples where one parent is overly responsible while the other is uninvolved or even abdicates. Even well-connected couples can feel alone in this battle if no one around them has been through this or seems to understand. We can have many good relationships, but those connections may or may not be particularly helpful when navigating teen grief.

As a parent, what can you do?

1. **Take care of yourself.**

   You are one of your teen's greatest assets in life. The healthier you are - physically, emotionally, and spiritually - the better able you will be to love and support your teen.

   Do what you need to do. Get good nutrition. Hydrate well. Exercise appropriately. Get regular medical check-ups. Seek intellectual and spiritual health. Take the next obvious, small step, whatever that is.

   Take good care of you. You're no good to your teen if you don't.

2. **If you're married, take care of your marriage.**

   Put time and energy into connecting deeply with your partner. The better your relationship is, the more your teen will benefit.

   Hurting teens need parents who are on the same page. If you want to love and support your teen better, focus on loving and supporting your partner well.

3. **Be involved in your teen's life (as much as they will let you).**

   Sounds obvious, but we all know this isn't necessarily easy. Let them know you're there. Ask questions in engaging, non-threatening, and non-intrusive ways. Ask because you love them and are genuinely interested, not because you want to know what they're thinking so that you can somehow control situations and their behavior.

   Make yourself available. Listen, listen, and listen some more. Be involved. As much as possible, meet them where they are and love them there.

4. **When you have a loss, grieve openly and in front of them, as appropriate.**

   Our kids need to know that we have hearts. We hurt and grieve too, and it's good for them to see this. We can model for them how to be authentic and grieve in healthy, positive ways. This has more power than we realize.

   Teens are watching. Be real. Be honest. Don't be afraid to grieve in front of them.

5. **Reach out and marshal some good resources.**

   By resources, I mean people. Friends, teachers, coaches, counselors, spiritual mentors, medical doctors, etc. We need a diverse team of helpful, supportive people to walk with us through this uncharted territory. For more info on this, see our discussion about a Grief Recovery Team in chapter nine.

   Don't go this alone. Surround yourself with supportive people who possess the abilities and skills to help.

6. **Be patient, with your teen and yourself.**

   Grief isn't an item you can check off a list. It's an ongoing, marathon-like process. It takes time and effort. There is no timetable for grief and grieving. You're in this for the long haul.

   You're not God. You're their parent. Be patient with yourself and them.

This is tough. Parenting may be one of the world's most challenging responsibilities. It's an honor.

Breathe deeply.

Love them.

You can make more of a difference than you think.

FOR PERSONAL REFLECTION AND/ OR GROUP DISCUSSION:

Which of the six suggestions in this chapter seems the most challenging for you at present? What makes this one difficult?

Of the six suggestions, which is the next most challenging for you, and why?

What action do you want to take next as a result of this chapter?

Don't worry about being perfect. Focus on being authentic and loving.

Help us reach and encourage more parents
and grandparents of grieving teens.
Share this link: https://www.garyroe.com/teengrief/

We're here to help. Together, we can make a difference.
If you need grief support, please visit us at www.garyroe.com.

CHAPTER 17
FOR TEACHERS AND COACHES

IF YOU'RE A TEACHER OR a coach, the influence you have in teen lives is extraordinary.

I grew up in an environment of abuse, mental illness, and emotional instability. When I started school, it was as if someone pumped oxygen into my soul. Teachers and coaches made a profound impact on my heart and life.

Mrs. Thomas was kind and encouraging. Her smile put me at ease. My heart began to relax a little.

Mrs. McShan got me excited about learning. I don't know how, but she made math my favorite subject.

Mr. Rainey was my first male teacher. His knowledge inspired me. He sensed things were not right at home, and quietly checked on me, asking how I was and how life was treating me.

Mrs. Richardson taught English and instilled in me a fascination for words. Little did I know how important that was going to become in my life.

Coach Elliott was my junior high tennis coach. He somehow made those awkward two years bearable. I can still his voice saying, "Good job, Roe."

Mrs. Wiggly was known for excellence and fair-mindedness. My first day back after my dad's death, she caught my eye and smiled. "Gary, if you need extensions on anything, please come talk to me. I'm so sorry about your dad." I didn't need any extensions (the work was good for my soul), but her caring words penetrated deep.

Then there were my swim coaches - Coaches Pickle, Tate, and Rogers. The impact these men made in my life was incalculable. I was around them more than any other adult growing up. They imparted to me mental and physical discipline, a powerful work ethic, and the will to endure adversity and persevere. I trusted them, and they were present at critical times in my young life.

When my dad died, almost every teacher and coach who knew me either came to the funeral or expressed their condolences. For the three remaining years of my high school career, they watched out for me. For all I knew, they were talking and working together to make sure I survived. I spent roughly 12 hours a day at school or in school-related athletics or activities (not counting homework!). These teachers and coaches became surrogate parents and influential mentors that helped shape the course of my thinking, education, and life. They helped keep me alive, safe, and stable.

Teachers and coaches, please don't ever underestimate your influence. Your presence, your attitude, your words, and your actions have a profound and lasting impact. You matter in teen lives, more than you realize.

Here are ways you can continue to make a positive difference in a hurting teen's life:

1. **Be aware that they are hurting, and most likely confused and angry.**

   Know that their losses are difficult for them to navigate. They need you.

2. **If you know in time, show up at the funeral of their loved one.**

   This will speak volumes. Your presence is incredibly powerful.

3. **Let them know that you know about their loss.**

Express your personal condolences in a way that fits your relationship with them.

4. **Express your availability, but don't make promises you can't keep.**

If you want to be there for them, let them know this. "My door is open." "If you want to talk, I'm here." "If I can help, let me know."

5. **Remember them at special times like Christmas, Thanksgiving, academic honors ceremonies, athletic banquets, and graduation.**

At special times like these, teens are hyper-aware of who's missing. You can help fill that void by simply telling them congratulations somehow. Express that you're proud of them. Your affirmation will sink deep into their hearts.

6. **Consider coordinating support with other faculty, parents, and mentors.**

Solid, caring adults can provide the stability a wounded teen needs to pilot through life's more troubling waters.

You are heroes to many teens. They look up to you. A kind look or an encouraging word from you might be the fuel that gets them through any particular day. Your presence in their lives is not coincidence or random. You chose your vocation. Chances are your love for kids led you into it. Thank you.

Teach.

Coach.

Affirm.

Encourage.

Meet teens where they are and love them there.

You are making more of a difference than you know.

FOR PERSONAL REFLECTION AND/ OR GROUP DISCUSSION:

What are some ways you can express condolences and concern for teens during a time of loss?

How might you connect with others to provide a wider support network for hurting teens?

Of the six suggestions in this chapter, which one strikes you the most? Explain.

Meet your teens where they are and love them there.
You're making more of a difference than you realize.

Please help us help teens by reaching more teachers and coaches.
Share this link: https://www.garyroe.com/teengrief/

Thank you for making a difference!
If you ever need grief support, we're here – www.garyroe.com

CHAPTER 18

FOR SOCIAL WORKERS, SCHOOL COUNSELORS, AND YOUTH ADVOCATES

S OCIAL WORKERS, SCHOOL COUNSELORS, AND community youth advocates...

If you fit in any of these categories, I want you to know that I admire you deeply. You've rolled up your sleeves and are willing to get dirty. You have laid down your lives for the benefit of others. Your days are about giving, protecting, and helping others, many of whom are compromised, needy, at-risk, and vulnerable. You are defenders, advocates, and healers. Your role in our society and world is crucial and indispensable. It's tough, demanding, and exhausting work. And it's worth it.

There are times when you may not see the changes that you work so hard to produce. You see heartbreaking situations where nothing good seems to emerge. Strange, difficult, abusive, violent, and evil things happen all around you. You put on your armor, marshal your heart and skills, and go battle for others, day after day.

Thank you.

You are making a difference - more than you can know or imagine. You're touching teen lives, hearts, and souls. This is hard, complicated, and intricate stuff. You don't have to understand it all. You show up, ready to face what comes across your desk or through your door.

Here are some suggestions for you, which I'm certain you already know:

1. **Be yourself.**

   Teens smell fake a mile away. Be real and authentic. They need the real you.

2. **Take care of yourself.**

   You are such a dedicated and devoted helper that this usually slips down on your priority list. You're too valuable and too important. Keep self-care at the top of your agenda. The better care you take of you, the more you can offer others.

3. **Meet teens where they are and do what you can, but also know your limits.**

   Most of you are extraordinarily hard on yourselves. Saving the world is not your job. Your calling is to touch those who are wounded and hurting and influence the world more toward compassion and healing.

   Don't expect yourself to be God. Be you instead.

4. **Think "team" and network continually.**

   Every teen needs a team - a diverse group of people with different experiences and skills. Do your part, and do what you can to get others involved. Don't try to be the sole resource. Be yourself, know your limits, and marshal other resources to meet other needs.

5. **Think outside the box and be a trailblazer.**

   "We've always done it this way" is not a good reason to keep doing it that way. Be creative.

   How can we better meet hurting teens where they are and be with them in their stuff?

   How can we better serve them and surround them with the team they need to recover, adjust, heal, and grow?

What needs to be changed, altered, or morphed to better connect with teens and their hearts?

6. **Listen, listen, listen.**

Even we helpers are prone to giving answers and fixing. Answers are important, but nothing beats listening. If teens feel heard, they begin to trust. When they feel safe and loved, healing and growth become possible.

It all begins with listening. Tune your ears to their hearts.

Thank you again for giving your life to assist and support others. Thank you for being compassionate and courageous. The world needs you. Teens need you.

FOR PERSONAL REFLECTION AND/ OR GROUP DISCUSSION:

Of the six suggestions in this chapter, which one is the most challenging for you? What makes this one difficult?

Of these six suggestions, which one do you feel most confident about in your role with teens? Describe why.

Are there any changes you want to attempt or make as a result of this chapter and this book? If so, describe them.

Be yourself. Meet teens where they are. Know your limits. Take good care of yourself. Don't underestimate the impact you can have.

Help teens by helping us reach more professionals like you.
Share this link: https://www.garyroe.com/teengrief/

Thank you for your commitment and service!
If you ever need grief support, we're here – www.garyroe.com

CHAPTER 19
FOR CLERGY AND SPIRITUAL MENTORS

I F YOU ARE A PASTOR, minister, Sunday School teacher, youth worker, or spiritual mentor, you deal in the realm of the sacred all day, every day. Every person you see is unique, created in the image of God, and of priceless, eternal value. You encounter their whole person - body, mind, soul, and spirit. Dealing on the soul level with spiritual matters is a great honor and privilege. It's humbling and can be unnerving at times.

Teens are searching. They are on an incessant quest to discover who they are, what life is all about, what love is and how to find it, and how to fit in and manage the tasks of daily life. Overall, their main concern is most likely how to survive the current jungle they find themselves immersed in. Self-worth, identity, relationships, family, acceptance, meaning, and purpose all seem to be at stake, every moment of every day. Almost everything seems urgent.

In times of loss, many teens are wondering...

"Where is God in all this?"

"Is God good?"

"Does God care?"

"Does he care about me?"

Teens are searching, and we are the answer-people, or so many believe. Teens don't find truth by being told. They are exposed to it, led into it, and then discover it for themselves. Our main goal is not to provide answers, but to help them ask the right questions. We're not here to fix what we see as their spiritual issues or problems. Our task is to meet them where they are and love them there.

Jesus entered our world and walked with us. We get to enter the teen's world and walk with them.

Here are some suggestions on how to do that when the teen is grieving:

1. **Be real and authentic.**

   Teens have amazing radar. They can detect "fake" in an instant. Be yourself. Stay down to earth. Don't get all super-spiritual on them. Speak their language, in your own way. Let it be about them, and not about your need to be of assistance or help.

2. **Listen, listen, and listen some more.**

   The teen is asking, "Are you for real? Do you care?" Restrain yourself and set your heart to hear and listen.

3. **Learn to ask questions before giving answers.**

   Simple questions can be the best. "How are you doing?" "What's this like for you? It has to be very difficult." "How can I be of the most help to you?"

4. **Be aware of things NOT to say.**

   Here are some examples I have heard that don't help at times like this:

   - "At least they're in a better place." "At least they're not suffering." "At least, you had them for this long."

     The statement, "At least..." though it might be true, ends up minimizing their loss and demeaning their personal grief and pain.

   - "It's God's will. We need to accept it."

   Personally, I don't believe everything that happens is the

will of God. That would make God the author of evil. Much suffering naturally occurs as the result of living in an imperfect and broken world. More of my thoughts on this can be found in the next chapter.

A friend of mine once said, "Everything that comes out of our mouths should be true, but not everything that is true should necessarily come out of our mouths." We get to speak truth with love. Love constrains what we say, and how.

As much as possible, let your words to grieving teens be governed by two questions: "Is it true?" and "It is loving right now?"

5. **Ask God to empower you to meet teens in their grief and feel some of it with them.**

There are times when God may deliver us from loss and pain, but most often he meets us in our distress and walks with us through it. By showing up and entering their mess with them, we can help teens realize that God too cares for them and is with them in their grief.

6. **Make yourself available, and pray a lot!**

Make yourself available to the teen, if you're willing. Check in with them regularly. Send them a simple text from time to time. "Thinking about you." "Praying for you." Even if they never respond, your contact can be the vehicle God uses to express his kindness and love. Pray for them, and keep on praying.

Don't try to be God. You won't succeed. Be yourself. Be who God made you. You are a fellow struggler who has also been wounded and grieves from time to time. Join teens as an equal, who happens to have a little more experience.

The impact you can have is stunning. You may never know or

see the results of your efforts. Have no agenda except to love them, and you can't help but succeed.

FOR PERSONAL REFLECTION AND/ OR GROUP DISCUSSION:

Of the six suggestions in this chapter, which one resonates the most with you? How so?

Of these six suggestions, which one seems to be the most difficult for you at present? What is it that makes this one so challenging?

At this point, what step can you take to better support hurting teens and their families?

Meet grieving teens where they are and have no agenda except to love them. You can't help but succeed.

Help us reach more clergy, parents, teachers, coaches, counselors, and youth workers. Share this link: https://www.garyroe.com/teengrief/

Thank you for your dedication and service. If you or anyone in your congregation ever needs grief support, we're here to serve you – www.garyroe.com

SUMMARY OF PART THREE

THE TEENAGE YEARS ARE VOLATILE. Cumulative grief from early childhood losses plus additional distress from current challenging or traumatic situations can place severe stress on an already embattled teen heart and mind. Teens are incredibly special people. They are the future. Each one is of priceless value, unique in human history. It's an honor to know them and walk through this time with them.

As parents, teachers, coaches, counselors, social workers, advocates, clergy, and mentors, we all fill unique and special roles in teens' lives. They are watching and listening more than we realize. They are looking for models – people to follow and emulate as they journey through their current minefield of loss and grief. We can be real, honest, and authentic, showing them how to grieve in healthy and ultimately productive ways. Taking good care of ourselves can often be the best thing we can do for the teens around us.

As we become more focused on living well with greater purpose and meaning, we are automatically encouraging teens to do the same. We're all in this together. Though our losses are not the same, we can still walk together, caring for and supporting each other in difficult times.

What happens to and around us is important. How we view and interpret what happens shapes our responses and future. It's not what happened or what we did then, but what we do next that matters most now.

Teens are designed for relationship and created for impact. So are we. Together, we can make more of a difference than any of us can imagine.

CHAPTER 20

A PERSONAL PERSPECTIVE
ON GRIEF AND LOSS

"Mourn with those who mourn."

– The Apostle Paul

T HANK YOU FOR YOUR CONCERN for teens and for taking the time and energy to read this book. I hope you found it informative, helpful, and practical. Grief is universal. We all experience it. Our losses are all unique, which makes grief a lonely road. But we can still walk it together.

I wanted to conclude by sharing my personal perspective on grief, loss, and healing. I do this in hopes that somehow my thoughts and experience might be beneficial to you in your journey with teens through this emotional, mental, physical, and spiritual minefield.

I AM A FELLOW STRUGGLER

As I mentioned in the introductory chapter, I am a fellow struggler. I have not arrived. I haven't figured this grief thing out. I tussle daily with issues stemming from the losses I have endured and continue to face. I trip and stumble frequently, but hopefully, I'm falling forward along the way.

I am a follower of Jesus Christ. I'm inconsistent, far from perfect, and downright weak at times. I'm often confused, frustrated, and more anxious than I would like to admit. I am a walking, breathing mass of contradictions. But Jesus is my life, and this influences what I think, do, and say - and how I write.

If you come from a different faith orientation or perhaps claim no particular faith at all, my goal here is not to offend you or cause you distress. Far from it. My purpose is to share what has been personally helpful to me in navigating this up-and-down existence of multiple losses in the hope that it will be beneficial to you as well.

So please take the following for what it is - my story. Your story is your own.

MY EARLY STORY

I lost both grandfathers very early. I hardly remember anything about either one of them. Due to dementia, one grandmother never knew who I was. Though I had many relatives nearby, my nuclear family was isolated and relationally distant from them. I remember feeling sad and lonely most of the time.

I lost large chunks of early childhood to repetitive and traumatic sexual abuse. This greatly shaped my view of myself, others, the world, and God. My sadness and loneliness grew. I went internal. During this time my brother, who was already in college, lost a girlfriend in a car accident and a classmate in Vietnam. The atmosphere of grief that permeated our home was heavy and stifling. It had a tinge of hopelessness to it.

When I was 12, a good school buddy died suddenly of spinal meningitis over the Christmas holidays. He sat in front of me in homeroom. The rest of the school year, I began each school day by staring at his empty desk. He was smart, fun, full of promise, and healthy. How could things like this happen?

My parents' marriage was not a peaceful one. They separated

and then divorced in my early teens. By default, I stayed with Mom. She had ongoing mental health issues which no one seemed to know what to do with. Day by day, she slipped deeper into a world of delusion. It was not a good situation. I moved in with Dad.

The next six months were some of the best of my life. I was 15 and felt like I was finally getting my feet under me. Dad was stable, and his presence provided a strong sense of safety. Then one Sunday afternoon, he collapsed in front of me of a massive heart attack. He never regained consciousness, and died a week later. My world, as I knew it, was over.

Reluctantly, I moved back in with Mom, who was even more unstable than before. Several months later, she attempted to take her own life. As she went into psychiatric care in the local hospital, it struck me that for all practical purposes I was an orphan.

Every loss, every death, has other losses, other little deaths, attached to it. The hits accumulate. My collateral damage was at such a point that my recollection of this time is garbled. I have memory gaps. Grief does that to us.

Life was not what I thought or hoped it would be. It was full of surprises, most of which seemed unwelcome and painful. I wondered where the next hit was going to come from.

Then something deep within me began to surface. A resolve. Something in my heart was tired of this. I wanted to fight.

In my simple teenage way, I accepted reality. Life was going to be hard. Bad stuff was going to happen. I was not in control of this. I did not have much say (if any) in what happened to me or around me.

At that point, I made two decisions. First, I resolved to bring as little distress on myself as possible. I was going to keep my nose clean, live well, and create as few disasters as I could. Second, I resolved to face grief and loss head-on, to fight, and to heal. Abuse, death, and collateral damage would not win.

About this time, I was taken in by the family of my best friend.

They already had four kids, and adding an at-risk kid like me to the mix was potentially dangerous. But they did it anyway.

This family loved me as their own son. They accepted and supported me in every way possible. I went through the days pinching myself, wondering if this could possibly be real. It was so good, in fact, that I simply couldn't take it all in.

One afternoon, I entered the dad's office and sat down in front of his desk. I asked why in the world he would take in a kid like me and make me a part of his family. He smiled, leaned forward, and said, "Gary, with what Jesus Christ did for us, how could we not do this for you?"

Something clicked in my heart. Jesus was not new to me. I began going to church when I was ten. I was hurting and looking for hope. I was introduced to Jesus there. I wasn't interested in religion. I needed love and relationship.

Now, here he was again, this Jesus.

I walked out of my new dad's office that day with a new sense of meaning and purpose. I launched on a lifelong journey to heal from the past. I wanted to live a different kind of life.

AN ADVENTURE OF HEALING

I entered college and studied Psychology. I immersed myself in service and found myself continually surrounded by troubled, grieving, and wounded people - people like me. Ever since, my adult life has revolved around helping hurting people heal and grow, finding greater perspective and healing for myself along the way.

As I got older, the losses continued to pile up, as they do with all of us. In addition, as a missionary and pastor, I was frequently around pain, grief, and loss. Now as a hospice chaplain and grief counselor, I'm in the presence of death every day. Grief is part of the air I breathe.

So many are hurting. Different people with diverse backgrounds, unique relationships, deeply personal losses, and different faiths.

But we all have this in common: we are human, and we experience loss.

I believe God knows our pain. More than this, I believe he feels it.

I believe he created us in his image, which means we are of priceless, eternal value, designed to reflect him. We're wired for relationship, to love and be loved. We don't do separation well. Our hearts break and shatter. God knows this. He walks with us in the valley of the shadow of death, though many times we are unaware of his presence.

Then there is this Jesus character. The Bible declares him to be God who has taken on human flesh. He came among us and experienced the joy, delight, and love that quality relationships can bring. He also tasted the ugliness of injustice, deception, manipulation, rejection, betrayal, abuse, torture, and violent death. No one truly understood him. He knows about loneliness. He is well acquainted with grief.

If he is God in human flesh, believing that he rose from the dead isn't a stretch for me. Rather, it seems plausible and natural. I believe he conquered death to offer me something better than the disappointment, pain, frustration, and loss of this world. I think he still conquers death, every day, in my life and in the lives of others.

Jesus knows. He knows grief, and he knows me. He shares my loneliness.

This companion has made all the difference for me. He shows up in unexpected and fascinating ways. He brings the right people at the right time and loves me through them. His presence is constant. He continually reminds me this is not all there is. Death has been conquered.

I still have questions. I have doubts periodically, even about his goodness. I get mad at him occasionally. He accepts me where I am. He loves me. He gets it.

Again, this is my story. My prayer is that it brings some comfort and hope to you as you encounter loss and pain in your own life and in the lives of the teens around you. Wounds and pain need not define our lives. If we're willing to grieve and heal, even devastating losses can be turned around and used for extraordinary good.

I close with something Jesus himself said that has been profoundly comforting to me. I hope you will find it so too.

"I have told you these things, so that in me you may have peace.
In this world, you will have trouble.
But take heart. I have overcome the world."

(Matthew 11:28-30)

Yes, we will have trouble. We all know this. Much of life, perhaps the majority, seems to be about overcoming. Every day is an extraordinary opportunity to take what seems (and many times is) devastating and use it for great, even eternal, good. For me, Jesus, the Overcomer, is key to all this.

So, here's to overcoming – today, tomorrow, and the day after that. As we do, the teens around us will take notice. Be the best you possible. Model being an overcomer. Give them something to shoot for.

You're more important than you know…

For more information about who Jesus is and what that might mean for your life, grief process, and healing, please visit www.garyroe.com/jesus-grief-and-healing.

TO YOU, FROM THE GRIEVING TEENAGE HEART

KATIE

Thank you for walking with me. You make such a difference in my life.

I'm living again, thanks to you and a few others. You stayed with me. You accepted me. You loved me where I was, and walked with me in my stuff. You were with me when I couldn't stand myself. I pushed you away, but you kept coming back.

Just knowing you're there helps me feel safe. And when I feel safe, my heart settles. Somehow, I believe things are going to be okay. I'm going to be okay.

I know I act like I understand everything. I understand hardly anything. But I can't afford to admit that. I'm an actress. I guess we all are. Maybe, with the help of people like you, I can learn to be more real.

I want to be real. I want to make a difference. I want to count.

I matter. I believe that now - because I mattered to you.

Thank you.

JOSH

I'm not good at saying thank you, so consider this a verbal fist-bump.

I'm still standing.

I'm still alive.

And I want to live.

You stood with me. You were there. You were a safety net. I act tough and independent, but I'm more brittle than I look. I'm mostly bravado. Somehow, I think you knew that.

I don't see oxygen, but I'm alive because of it. I breathe in invisible stuff, and live. You're kind of like that. I don't always see you, but I know you're there.

I don't know how all this is going to turn out, but I now believe I'm going to be okay, somehow, some way. The world needs more people like you. I hope I run into them. I want to be one of those people for someone else. Maybe I will be.

Thanks for seeing me through this and for giving me something to shoot for.

Verbal fist-bump...

HINTS FOR GROUP
DISCUSSION

"**C**AN I USE THIS BOOK in a group? If so, how?"
Great question. The answer is, "Yes!" Here are some guidelines.

GROUND RULES

I'm assuming your group would be made of parents living with grieving teens or others who work with youth.

First, make sure your group is clear on its purpose and rules of interaction. Here are some group ground rules you can read out loud at the beginning of each group meeting.

GROUP GROUND RULES

We're here because we live (or work) with hurting, grieving teens. We want to make a positive and healing difference in their lives.

To get the most out of this group, we need to be able to share freely. We need to feel safe.

As a result, here are our ground rules:

1. What is shared here is confidential. What is said in the group stays in the group.

2. We will not try to fix or help each other feel better. There is no fixing this.

3. We will not give advice unless someone specifically asks for input.

4. We will not compare our teens or their losses. There is no "easier," "harder," "better," or "worse," but only "different."

5. Each person is free to share. Each person is free not to share.

6. We will respect each other by being careful not to dominate, giving others a chance to share their story.

Having good, clear ground rules sets the tone for a good group.

TIME, PACING, AND DURATION

Second, if you're wanting to use *Teen Grief* in a support group, I would recommend having people read two chapters a week. At that pace, it would take 8-10 weeks to move through the book, depending on which of the final chapters you decide to include for discussion.

I would recommend your group meet weekly (continuity is important) for an hour and a half. This gives people a chance to settle, share, and support each other. Often the time after the group is equally valuable. Just being together can be profoundly helpful and healing.

SAMPLE QUESTIONS FOR GROUP MEETINGS

You can simply work through the personal reflection and group discussion questions at the end of each chapter. If you need additional questions, you can try supplementing with one or two of these:

- What struck you the most in the "From the Grieving Teenage Heart" sections you read this week?

- What do you sense was the most important thing you learned this week?

- Is there something specific you want to try this week to support your grieving teen?

Remember that your group is about people's hearts and lives and not simply about getting through the material. Give the group direction. Be okay with silence, and yet keep them moving. Be intentional, and yet flexible. There is no "perfect" here. If you lead in a compassionate and loving way, you can bet those attending (and their teens) will benefit.

Both leading and participating in groups takes courage. You are braver than you know. Our teens are worth it. You are worth it. Those around you are worth it.

CARING FOR GRIEVING HEARTS

Visit Gary at www.garyroe.com and connect with him
on Facebook, Twitter, LinkedIn, and Pinterest

Links:
Facebook: https://www.facebook.com/garyroeauthor
Twitter: https://twitter.com/GaryRoeAuthor
LinkedIn: https://www.linkedin.com/in/garyroeauthor
Pinterest: https://www.pinterest.com/garyroe79/

ADDITIONAL RESOURCES

BOOKS

COMFORT FOR GRIEVING HEARTS: HOPE AND ENCOURAGEMENT FOR TIMES OF LOSS

We look for comfort. We long for it. Grieving hearts need it to survive. Written with heartfelt compassion, this easy-to-read, warm, and practical book reads like a caring conversation with a friend and is destined to become a classic for those looking for hope and encouragement in times of loss. Composed of brief chapters, **Comfort for Grieving Hearts** is designed to be read one chapter per day, giving you bite-sized bits of comfort, encouragement, and healing over time. Available through Amazon and most major online retailers. For more information or to download a free excerpt, visit www.garyroe.com.

SHATTERED: SURVIVING THE LOSS OF A CHILD

Unthinkable. Unbelievable. Heartbreaking. Whatever words we choose, they all fall far short of the reality. The loss of a child is a terrible thing. How do we survive this? Written at the request of grieving parents and grandparents, **Shattered** has been called "one of the most comprehensive and practical grief books available."

The book combines personal stories, compassionate guidance, and practical suggestions/exercises designed to help shattered hearts navigate this devastating loss. **Shattered** became an Amazon #1 Bestseller soon after its publication and has received sterling reviews by both mental health professionals and grieving parents. It is available in both paperback and electronic versions on Amazon and most other major online book retailers.

PLEASE BE PATIENT, I'M GRIEVING: HOW TO CARE FOR AND SUPPORT THE GRIEVING HEART

People often feel misunderstood, judged, and even rejected during a time of loss. This makes matters more difficult for an already broken heart. It doesn't have to be this way. It's time we took the grieving heart seriously. Gary wrote this book by request to help others better understand and support grieving hearts, and to help grieving hearts understand themselves. A group discussion guide is included. **Please Be Patient, I'm Grieving** became a #1 Amazon Bestseller soon after its release and was honored as a 2016 Best Book Awards Finalist. It can be found in both paperback and electronic formats on Amazon and most other major online bookstores.

HEARTBROKEN: HEALING FROM THE LOSS OF A SPOUSE

Losing a spouse is painful, confusing, and often traumatic. This comforting and practical book was penned from the stories of dozens of widows and widowers. It's simple, straightforward approach has emotionally impacted hearts and helped thousands know they're not alone, not crazy, and that they will make it. An Amazon Top 10 Bestseller, **Heartbroken** was a 2015 USA Best Book Award Finalist and a National Indie Excellence Book Award Finalist. Available in paperback and electronic formats from Amazon and most major online retailers.

SURVIVING THE HOLIDAYS WITHOUT YOU: NAVIGATING LOSS DURING SPECIAL SEASONS

This warm and intensely practical volume has been dubbed a "Survival Kit for Holidays." It has helped many understand why holidays are especially hard while grieving and how to navigate them with greater confidence. Being proactive and having a plan can make all the difference. An Amazon holiday bestseller, *Surviving the Holidays Without You* was a 2016 Book Excellence Award Finalist. Available in paperback and electronic formats on Amazon and most major online retailers.

SAYING GOODBYE: FACING THE LOSS OF A LOVED ONE

Full of stories, this warm, easy-to-read, and beautifully illustrated gift book has comforted thousands. It reads like a conversation with a close friend, giving wise counsel and hope to those facing a loss. Co-authored with *New York Times' Bestseller* Cecil Murphey, this attractive hardback edition is available at www.garyroe.com/saying-goodbye

FREE ON GARY'S WEBSITE

THE GOOD GRIEF MINI-COURSE

Full of personal stories, inspirational content, and practical assignments, this 8-session mini-course is designed to help readers understand grief and deal with its roller-coaster emotions. Several thousand have been through this course, which is now being used in support groups as well. Available at https://www.garyroe.com/good-grief-mini-course/.

THE HOLE IN MY HEART: TACKLING
GRIEF'S TOUGH QUESTIONS

This powerful e-book tackles some of grief's big questions: "How did this happen?" "Why?" "Am I crazy?" "Am I normal?" "Will this get any easier?" plus others. Written in the first person, it engages and comforts the heart. Available at https://www.garyroe.com/the-hole-in-my-heart/

I MISS YOU: A HOLIDAY SURVIVAL KIT

Thousands have downloaded this brief, easy-to-read, and very personal e-book. *I Miss You* provides some basic, simple tools on how to use holiday and special times to grieve well and love those around you. Available at https://www.garyroe.com/i-miss-you/

ABOUT THE AUTHOR

Gary's story began with a childhood of mixed messages and sexual abuse. This was followed by other losses and numerous grief experiences.

Ultimately, a painful past led Gary into a life of helping wounded people heal and grow. A former college minister, missionary in Japan, entrepreneur in Hawaii, and pastor in Texas and Washington, he now serves as a writer, speaker, chaplain, and grief counselor.

In addition to *Teen Grief*, Gary is the author of numerous books, including the award-winning bestsellers *Shattered: Surviving the Loss of a Child*, *Please Be Patient, I'm Grieving*, and *Heartbroken: Healing from the Loss of a Spouse*. He has been featured on Focus on the Family, Dr. Laura, Beliefnet, the Christian Broadcasting

Network, and other major media and has well over 500 grief-related articles in print. Recipient of the Diane Duncam Award for Excellence in Hospice Care, Gary is a popular keynote, conference, and seminar speaker at a wide variety of venues.

Gary loves being a husband and father. He has seven adopted children, including three daughters from Colombia. He enjoys hockey, corny jokes, good puns, and colorful Hawaiian shirts. Gary and his wife Jen and family live in Texas.

Visit Gary at www.garyroe.com.

Links:
Facebook: https://www.facebook.com/garyroeauthor
Twitter: https://twitter.com/GaryRoeAuthor
LinkedIn: https://www.linkedin.com/in/garyroeauthor
Pinterest: https://www.pinterest.com/garyroe79/

Download your free, printable PDF:
Truths for Supporting Grieving Teens
https://www.garyroe.com/19-truths-for-supporting-grieving-teens

AN URGENT PLEA
HELP OTHER GRIEVING HEARTS

Dear Reader,

Others are hurting and grieving today. You can help.

How?

With a simple, heartfelt review.

Could you take a few moments and write a 1-3 sentence review of *Teen Grief* and leave it on Amazon?

Just go find *Teen Grief* on Amazon and then click on "Customer Reviews" just under the title.

And if you want to help even more, you could leave the same review on the *Teen Grief* book page on Goodreads.

Your review counts and will help reach others who could benefit from this book. Thanks for considering this. I read these reviews as well, and your comments and feedback assist me in producing more quality resources for grieving hearts.

Thank you!

Warmly,

Gary